Painting
Nature's
Treasures

Kelly Hoernig

North Light Books
Cincinnati, Ohio
www.artistsnetwork.com

About the Author

Kelly Hoernig has a fine arts degree from the American Academy of Art in Chicago where she studied Architectural Rendering, Watercolor and Lettering. She worked in advertising and now designs for the decorative painting market. Being a member of the Society of Decorative Painters (SDP) and the Society of Craft Designers (SCD) has allowed her to develop and explore many avenues of designing. Establishing herself as a designer in the decorative painting market has taken her from exhibiting to teaching across the United States. Her designs can be found in many of the leading decorative painting and crafting magazines as well as in books from top-of-the-line publishers. She now enjoys painting, teaching and designing from her studio in a wonderful country setting.

To learn more:
The Society of Decorative Painters (SDP) The Society of Craft Designers (SCD)
www.decorativepainters.org   www.craftdesigners.org

09 08 07 06 05   5 4 3 2 1

Library of Congress Cataloging-in-Publication Data

Hoernig, Kelly
    Painting nature's treasures / Kelly Hoernig.
        p. cm.
    Includes index.
    ISBN 1-58180-591-8 (alk. paper)
    1. Acrylic painting--Technique. 2. Decoration and ornament.
    3. Painted woodwork. 4. House furnishings. I. Title

TT385.H64 2005
745.7'23--dc22
                                2004052087

Editor: Tonia Davenport
Designer: Leigh Ann Lentz
Layout Artists: Amy F. Wilkin and Camille DeRhodes
Production Coordinator: Kristen Heller
Photographers: Christine Polomsky and Tim Grondin
Photo Stylist: Nora Martini

METRIC CONVERSION CHART

TO CONVERT	TO	MULTIPLY BY
Inches	Centimeters	2.54
Centimeters	Inches	0.4
Feet	Centimeters	30.5
Centimeters	Feet	0.03
Yards	Meters	0.9
Meters	Yards	1.1
Sq. Inches	Sq. Centimeters	6.45
Sq. Centimeters	Sq. Inches	0.16
Sq. Feet	Sq. Meters	0.09
Sq. Meters	Sq. Feet	10.8
Sq. Yards	Sq. Meters	0.8
Sq. Meters	Sq. Yards	1.2
Pounds	Kilograms	0.45
Kilograms	Pounds	2.2
Ounces	Grams	28.4
Grams	Ounces	0.04

Dedication

This book is dedicated to my wonderful husband, John, who has helped me explore the wonderful world of art for over twenty-three years.

Acknowledgments

I would like to thank my students — Cassie, Helen, Becky, Jan and Mary — for pushing me to explore avenues out of my comfort zone.

I would also like to thank my North Light family — Tricia Waddell, for giving me this wonderful opportunity; Christine Doyle, for guiding me along the way; Tonia Davenport, for being so supportive and keeping me on track; Christine Polomsky, for making my photo shoot easy and fun; and all the members who are behind the scenes making things run smoothly.

Table of Contents

Planting the Seeds . . . 16

Add Water and Sunlight ...44

Enjoying the Harvest ...66

Introduction

This book was created to share my love of nature with its reader. Since moving to the country, I have taken it upon myself to enjoy each of nature's little treasures whenever I see one. You can be totally fascinated by your surroundings if you give them that second look and really focus on the details.

The motifs created in this book are truly quite easy to master with results both charming and detail oriented. Each item is shaded and highlighted, and if there is an easier way to achieve any effect, I've shown it to you. Simple details are what brings things to life. Leave no line just one color; that added dash of color can make the difference on a piece and it shows you took the time to make it correctly.

The exploration of texture is another area of this book that I want to bring to your attention. There is sponging using a sea sponge, a stencil sponge and compressed sponges. Stenciling, marbling and faux finishing will also be introduced. Adding texture is easy to do and enhances your artwork so much that it will grab the viewer's attention and won't let go. With these simple techniques, your artwork will be enriched beyond belief.

The projects will begin with a simple basecoated background and will slowly advance to include a background that uses a faux finishing technique. Take it one project at a time and you are sure to have the success I intended for the completed piece. The techniques are broken down with step-by-step photos, making them easy to follow. Once you learn the process, the rest is easy to do.

Don't be afraid to mix and match background techniques to create unique pieces of your own. I want you to have fun with these projects, maybe learn a little, but most of all, explore all the possibilities they provide.

So, grab your paints and brushes
and let the **creativity** begin!

Basic Materials

Before beginning the projects, it is worth going over a few basics, such as the supplies that will be used and some specific information about each.

Brushes

There are several sizes and types of brushes that you will want to have to create the projects in this book. Each brush has a special shape that makes it easy for you to paint a specific stroke or texture. I prefer to use only Loew-Cornell brushes for their dependable quality, but if you have a different preference in a manufacturer, any brand will work fine. The size and shape are what is most important. For information on using these brushes, see pages 11–15.

1-inch (25mm) Wash Basecoater
Most projects begin with a solid basecoat of paint, and this size brush allows you to quickly cover your surface.

¾-inch (19mm) Wash
I use this brush more than any other. It is great for basecoating individual elements and for floating in all areas.

No. 4 Round Stroke
Round brushes, such as this one, have a full load of bristles that taper to a pointed end. This brush will be used for some of the detail work.

⅜-inch (10mm) DM Stippler
The filaments in this brush are a bit stiffer than in some of the other brushes. It is used to add a stippled or dappled texture and shading.

Shader, various sizes
These brushes have a flat or chisel edge. Their square shape creates crisp edges and provides control in tight areas. They are used to float and blend color.

No. 1 Liner
A liner is like a round brush, with fewer bristles and a slightly more pointed tip. It is used for making lines, as the name implies.

No. 1 Script Liner
This variety of liner has longer bristles than a regular liner, so it can hold more paint and make longer lines.

No. 6 Filbert
This flat brush is rounded at the end and it can be used to basecoat as well as make leaves.

Paints

For the projects in this book, acrylic paint in a variety of colors will be used. This type of paint dries quickly and cleans up easily with soap and water. I have used DecoArt Americana Acrylics in a limited palette of twenty-four (24) colors. Feel free to substitute any brand you like, but be sure the brand you choose is of good quality and that the manufacturer makes a wood sealer to go along with their paint.

Mediums

Along with acrylic paint, there are other mediums used for this book's projects. Look for these products in the same section as the paint.

Wood Sealer

A sealer creates a barrier between a porous surface, such as wood, and the paint, allowing the paint to adhere evenly. It also prevents moisture within the surface from leaking out into the paint.

Faux Glazing Medium

Using this DecoArt product allows the paint to become transparent, making various strengths of color. For the faux finishes, it enables you to have depth easily without a lot of work. I usually mix it in equal parts with the paint. Try varying the amount on your own palette to see the difference.

Varnish

Varnish is a sealant that creates a barrier between the painted surface and the air, protecting the surface from moisture and dirt. After the time spent painting a project, you want your surface to withstand the test of time.

Tools and Materials

Now that you're familiar with paints, brushes and mediums, let's take a look at some of the other supplies you'll need to make your painting experience a success.

Double-Ended Stylus

This tool is used to transfer a pattern to a surface using either graphite paper, white transfer paper or super chaco paper.

Scissors

You'll need these to cut shapes out of compressed sponges, as well as to trim the paper of your patterns down when necessary.

T-Square

A T-square will aid you in drawing lines that are perpendicular to one side of a box or frame. It is easier to use this type of ruler than measuring off two opposing sides to connect a line.

Toothbrush

An old toothbrush is a great tool for spattering paint onto a surface, giving it a speckled look.

Sanding Blocks and Paper

Sanding blocks work well to sand flat and larger surfaces, while curved or carved areas may require a flexible piece of sandpaper. Medium grit works best for initial sanding, while a finer grade, or brown kraft paper, works best for surfaces that have been given an initial basecoat.

Stencil Sponge

This type of sponge's wedge-shape is helpful for getting paint into the small detailed areas of a stencil.

Sea Sponge

A sea sponge creates a nicely irregular texture when used to apply paint to a surface.

Compressed Sponge

This type of sponge comes in a thin sheet, and allows you to create your own shape to stamp with. Simply cut out the shape with scissors and dip the shape in water to expand the sponge.

Wood Glue

This glue is water soluble and is the best way to bond one piece of wood to another, such as in the assembly of a stool or for adding wooden cutouts to a surface.

Glue Stick

Look for a glue stick that is acid free. It is used for adhering paper together.

Industrial Adhesive

This type of adhesive is water proof and is the best choice for adhering heavier objects or those with an uneven surface. I prefer E6000 for this type of glue. Due to the extreme vapors, always use in a well-ventilated area.

Transparent Tape

This tape is also known as Magic Tape. In this book it will be used for masking off areas before painting, rather than as an adhesive.

Palette Paper

This paper comes in a tablet form with disposable sheets. It is water-resistant and will hold enough puddles of paint to complete a project. I usually cut the tablet in half to make the size more convenient for my painting area.

Transfer Paper

Graphite paper and white transfer paper function the same way. The graphite variety shows up on a light-colored surface, while white is best for darker-colored surfaces. Both are smudge proof and erasable. Super chaco paper goes on blue and works on virtually any type of surface. Tracings are easily removed with a damp cloth or paper towel.

White Charcoal Pencil

Use this pencil to make marks or map out a design to be painted on your surface. It is easily removed with a damp cloth.

Plastic Wrap

In the last chapter of this book, we will use plastic wrap in conjunction with paint and a faux glazing medium to create a unique background texture on your surfaces.

Paper Towels

Not only are paper towels nice to have for cleanup, they are a great surface on which to pounce off excess paint from your stencil brushes and sponges. The most absorbent variety will save you money in the long run.

Brush Tub

This sectioned tub allows space for both dirty and clean water. The unique scrubbing sections will help you maintain quality brushes. Always scrub in one direction, not back and forth.

Basic Techniques

Now that you've been introduced to the basic materials and tools that will be used on the projects in the book, it's time to introduce some basic techniques. Following is an overview of using the various types of brushes as well as the necessary prep work for painting surfaces.

Preparing a Wood Surface

This is perhaps the most important part of your project, for it determines the overall quality and feel of your finished piece. It may be tempting to skip these steps, but if you take the time to prepare your surface properly, you'll be happier in the long run with the superior quality it produces.

1 Sand the Surface

Sand all sides of the wooden surface in the direction of the grain. Wipe away any sanding dust with a damp paper towel.

2 Mix Wood Sealer and Paint

Time is saved by mixing the wood sealer and the basecoat color together, rather than applying the sealer first and then a first coat of paint. Pour out an equal amount of both and mix them together with either a stylus or palette knife. Using a 1-inch (25mm) basecoater, cover the surface with the mixture, painting in the direction of the grain. This shortcut should only be taken when using the same brands of sealer and paint. If different brands are being used, apply sealer first, let dry and then basecoat with the paint.

3 Sand the Surface Again

Sand the entire surface again lightly to remove any grain that was raised in the basecoating. This step may also be completed with a paper bag. Follow with one more coat of just the basecoat color (no sealer added).

10

Getting Started

Once your surface is sanded, sealed and basecoated, you will be ready to start creating beautiful nature-inspired projects. Here are some tips for getting yourself set up.

Transferring a Pattern

Many patterns in this book are already printed at their actual size and the elements can be hand-traced onto tracing paper. For patterns that give direction to enlarge, make the enlargement on a photocopier, and print patterns onto vellum.

Align the vellum copy or traced elements over the surface to be painted and tape it down at the top. Slip graphite, white transfer or chacopaper between the surface and the pattern. Using the small end of the stylus, trace over the basic elements as lightly as you can, while still being able to see them. The details will be traced after the image has been basecoated.

Setting up Your Palette

Cut your palette paper in half to keep your paints neat and compact, and to conserve paper.

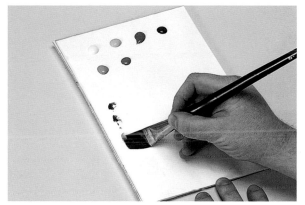

Squeeze out a small puddle of each color you will be using. Load your brush with color and walk it out down the left side of the palette (start on the right hand side, if you're left handed). This will give you little rows of color to more easily control the amount of paint you load on your brush.

Specialty Brushes

In addition to a basecoater brush and one or two flat brushes, here are four others that you will want to have on hand. Each one is made to allow you to create a specific stroke or shape.

Script Liner

The script liner brush is used to create long, continuous lines. It will travel farther than a regular liner because it holds more paint. Because you want it to give you long strokes, mix a bit of water into the paint to achieve an ink-like consistency. To load the script liner, dampen your brush, blot dry, then fully load with paint. The paint should be almost to the brush ferrule (metal part of the brush).

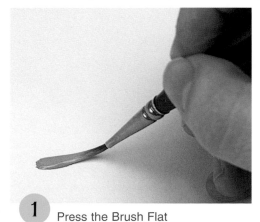

1 Press the Brush Flat

When doing a branch, start out with full pressure making the brush end press flat.

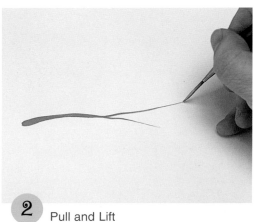

2 Pull and Lift

As you pull along, lift slightly with light pressure. For a consistent line, pull with even pressure looking slightly ahead to where you want the line to end up.

11

Liner

For fine liner work, add a little water to your brush. For heavier applications, dip into your paint puddle, then pull a line on your palette to remove any excess paint.

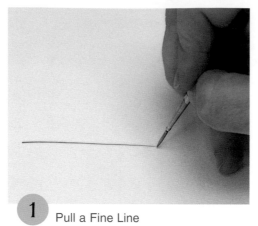

1 Pull a Fine Line

To achieve a fine line, stay on the tip of your brush.

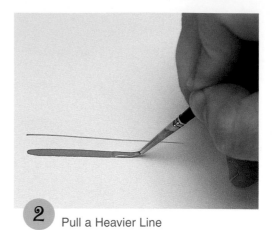

2 Pull a Heavier Line

For a heavier line, press the brush tip flat and pull with consistent pressure and movement.

Filbert

I love my filbert for making leaves, small comma strokes, bee wings, tail feathers and more. Once you learn how to use it, the possibilities will be endless. Fully load your filbert for the best results.

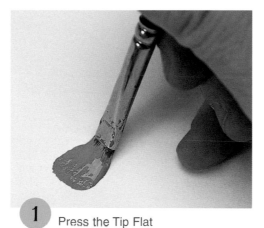

1 Press the Tip Flat

When it is loaded, begin by pressing the brush tip flat, then lift and twist.

2 Lift the Brush Up

For longer strokes you will press it flat, pull and lift, then end with a twist. For some strokes you just touch down and pull right back up.

DM Stippler

This brush is great for stippling because of its shape. Instead of being round, it is oval so you can load just a portion of it, giving you more control over where you place the color.

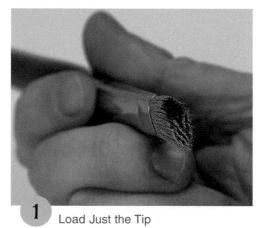

1 Load Just the Tip

Dampen the brush with water, blot dry, then load only one end of the brush tip. Pounce up and down onto your palette to remove excess paint.

2 Work the Color Down

Start with a full concentration of color and work your way down. Because this is a dampened brush, the water is actually helping you achieve a soft, gradated effect.

Basic Brush Strokes

The brush strokes used for the projects in this book are all very easy. Once you learn the basics that will be introduced here, you'll have the ability to create great projects that will amaze your friends and family. The same techniques will appear over and over again throughout the book.

Floating

This is a technique that uses a side-loaded brush and water to create a gradation from one side of the stroke to the other.

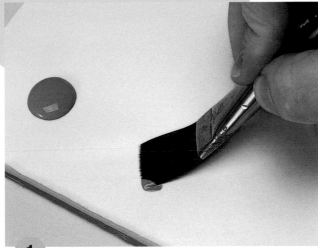

1 Load the Brush

When floating color, use the largest brush possible. Dampen the brush with water, then blot onto a paper towel. Dip a corner of the brush into the paint puddle, lay it flat onto the palette and wiggle. Flip the brush and do the same to the other side (not to the other end). It is now fully loaded and ready for floating.

2 Pull a Continuous Stroke

While using a large brush may seem scary at first, you will have better control and softer floats because of a greater brush surface area. See the long, continuous float the wider brush achieved versus the smaller brush.

3 Add a Shade

Shading is done in the shadow area and is always of a darker value. When floating on a basecoated image, I normally do the shading first. Start away from the edge about ⅛" (3mm), then push the float into the edge. This will help you create a wider float.

4 Add a Highlight

Highlighting is creating the lightest value placed on your project. Highlights are usually found on the top of an object or in the area where light would hit it. Here, a highlight color is floated in the same manner as a shade.

Walking Out a Loaded Brush

When walking out color, you are trying to establish a nice, wide float. It should be darker where you start and lighter toward the end.

Start at the end you want the deepest color and walk your brush toward the lighter end in even strokes. The water on your brush will smooth out the walking motion, giving you a wide, floated area.

Comma Stroke

A comma stroke is, as the name implies, a stroke that looks like a comma.
It will be used in this book to form flower petals, add texture to shells, make little leaves and more.

1 Press the Brush Flat

To make a comma stroke, dip the brush into paint, remove excess paint on your palette, then press flat.

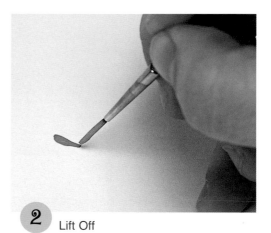

2 Lift Off

Now pull, twist and lift. Notice that you will end up on the tip of your brush with just the tip touching the surface—perfect!

Brush Mixing

When you need just a little bit of color, I suggest brush mixing instead of mixing up a whole new puddle of color on your palette paper. To do this, just dip your brush into one color and then the other, mix on your palette paper until blended, then paint onto your piece. It is a fast and easy way to do a small highlight or shade.

Adding a Textured Background

There are a couple of different techniques that can quickly add depth and texture to a basecoated background. Once you learn how easy these methods are, you'll want to experiment with different colors and brush sizes.

Slip-Slap

This is a wet-on-wet technique to give you a mottled, soft look. Wet-on-wet means just what it says, working on one wet layer while adding another.

Basecoat the area with one color and let dry. Basecoat again and while wet, quickly add the other colors and slip-slap the paint using a criss-cross motion until you get the overall appearance you want. If you prefer a smoother look, add a little more water to your brush for this step. I prefer the strokes to show in this application.

Spattering

This technique allows you to add an appealing, speckled texture to the background of your piece. Try experimenting with the thickness of the paint as well as different color combinations.

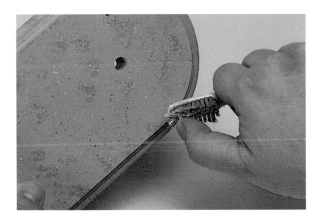

Use an old, stiff toothbrush to spatter. Wet it, blot on a paper towel, then dip a corner or tip into the paint puddle. By brushing your thumb or finger over the bristles quickly, you will get a nice spatter of paint. If the brush spatters where you didn't want it to, dampen a flat brush and remove the spatter while it's wet.

Finishing

Now that you've learned the basics for painting, here are a few things to help you finish and protect your projects properly.

- Erase any visible graphite lines using a soft white eraser. Wipe away eraser shavings with your hand or a dry brush.

- Always remember to sign your piece. I use a Micron Pigma Pen for this, but many artists use a color from the project palette and a liner brush. Do whatever you feel comfortable with; a regular graphite pencil works as well, and will last forever. Just be sure to seal it!

- Let your piece cure completely before varnishing. On a tin piece I like to let it sit at least 24 hours. In higher humidity, let it sit longer.

- Spray with several light coats of sealant, letting them dry adequately before applying the next layer. You should have three to five light coats when finished. With a brush-on varnish, follow the grain of the wood and let it dry before applying another layer.

PLANTING *the* SEEDS

*One tiny little seed can sprout a giant fern.
This section of the book is about getting our
feet wet and our hands dirty. It all begins with
the exploration of the most simple techniques.
We will lay down a foundation of color, then
explore the use of stencils and basic brush
strokes on both paper and wood to provide
you with a unique background for your artwork.*

*You will see how to create painted artwork
that looks like hand-stitched needlework,
how the addition of a wooden cutout gives
a piece dimension and how sponges can be
cut into shapes and then used to stamp paint
onto your surface.*

*With these basic seeds successfully planted, you
might surprise even yourself with the new ideas
you'll soon have growing in your head and the
plans you'll make to start something new.*

Caterpillar Chintz

The sophistication of chintz combined with the playfulness of this little caterpillar creates quite a unique piece. This project is very versatile because you can substitute any message or quote you'd like in the little frame.

Write in your heart that every day is the best day of the year.

Ralph Waldo Emerson

Materials

- wood frame
- bristol board, cut to fit the frame's image size
- computer-printed quote
- wood sealer
- no. 1 liner brush
- no. 2 flat brush
- no. 4 round stroke brush
- ⅜-inch (10mm) DM Stippler
- 1-inch (25mm) basecoater
- stencil sponge
- glue stick
- wood glue
- scissors
- ruler
- pencil
- stylus
- graphite paper
- chintz stencil
- caterpillar pattern (page 21)

DecoArt Americana Acrylic Paints

- Driftwood
- Light Buttermilk
- Mississippi Mud
- Raw Umber
- Reindeer Moss Green

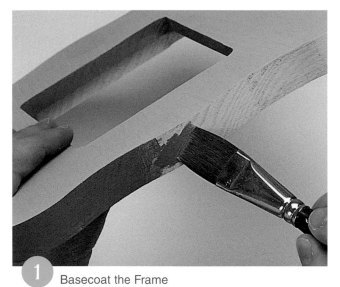

Basecoat the Frame

Prepare the frame surface with sealer and Reindeer Moss Green (see Preparing a Wood Surface, page 10). Basecoat the outer and inner edges of the frame with Mississippi Mud. Basecoat the dowel (stand) with Reindeer Moss Green.

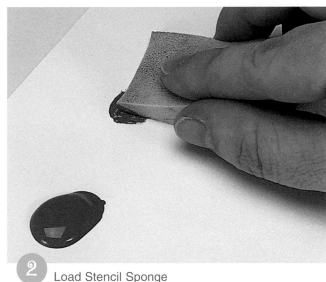

Load Stencil Sponge

Position the stencil so that the pattern is centered nicely on the wooden surface. Using a dry stencil sponge, dip the corner into Mississippi Mud and pounce onto the palette paper a few times to work in the paint.

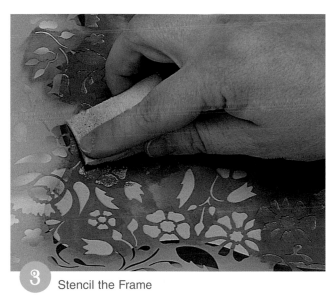

Stencil the Frame

Secure the stencil in one hand and begin pouncing the paint over the openings in the stencil, using even pressure. Redip the sponge when you feel yourself pressing extra hard to apply the paint. Be extra vigorous in the fine areas of the stencil to be sure paint gets to the surface. Before removing the stencil, lift and check to see that all of the design has been filled in. Rinse sponge in water and dab well on a paper towel to dry, before it is used again with a different color.

Stencil the Bristol Board

Place the piece of bristol board under the center, unpainted part of the stencil. Dip the sponge into the Reindeer Moss Green and dab off the excess. Holding the stencil with one hand, sponge over the stencil using a dabbing motion. Stenciling on paper requires a slightly drier sponge of loaded paint because the paint will bleed into the paper if it's too wet. Reloading the sponge will happen more frequently for the paper than it did for the wood. Don't worry about overlapping a little into the section of the stencil that was used on the frame.

Tip

A stencil sponge applies the paint a little less evenly than a stencil brush, giving more of a gently-shaded appearance.

5 Create Text Frame

Measure off the box for the quote, using a pencil. For a frame with a 4" × 6" (10cm × 15cm) opening, start 3¼" (8cm) from the left and ⅜" (1cm) down from the top and make a vertical box that is 1⅞" × 2⅞" (5cm × 7cm). Draw these lines lightly. Using graphite paper and the stylus, transfer the caterpillar pattern to the left of the box, so he appears to be climbing up the box. Basecoat the box with the no. 2 flat and Mississippi Mud. Thin the paint a bit with water so it will go on smoothly. Press the brush down firmly to ensure an even thickness throughout. With the same brush and color, basecoat the body of the caterpillar.

6 Add Caterpillar Feet

Add the feet to the caterpillar with Raw Umber and the no. 4 round stroke brush. Press the brush all the way down to form a square for the foot and then lift back up.

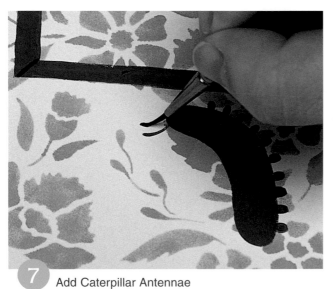

7 Add Caterpillar Antennae

With the liner and Raw Umber, make a comma stroke for the antennae. Starting away from the head, press down with the brush, then lift up in a swipe to form the shape (see Comma Stroke, page 14).

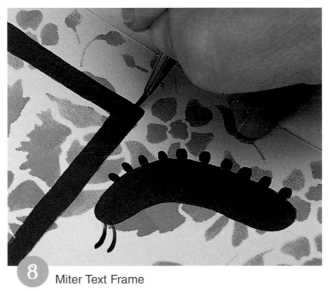

8 Miter Text Frame

With the liner brush, add a miter to each of the four corners of the text frame with Raw Umber.

9 Highlight and Shade Body

Use the ⅜-inch (10mm) DM Stippler brush to highlight the body of the caterpillar. Begin by dipping the brush in the water and blot dry on a paper towel. Dip only the tip (about one quarter) into Driftwood and pounce the highlights onto the top of the body. Shade along the bottom and the ends of the body with a float of Raw Umber.

10 Add Body Dots

Add dots of Reindeer Moss Green using the liner brush along the top of the body following its curve.

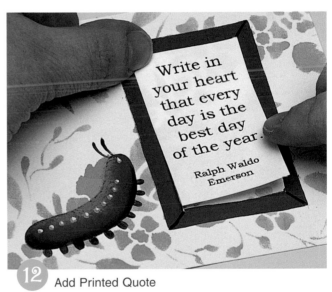

11 Highlight the Dots

Add a highlight dot of Light Buttermilk on top of the green dots.

12 Add Printed Quote

Using scissors, trim the computer-printed quote to 1½" × 2½" (4cm × 6cm). Adhere the quote with glue stick to the center of the painted frame. Glue in the dowel to the back of the frame, using wood glue. Sign your name, and apply sealant to finish (see tips on finishing, page 15). Adhere a second piece of bristol board to the back of the painted board for support, and place the finished piece into the frame.

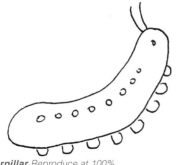

Caterpillar Reproduce at 100%

21

Notes on the Fly

When I saw this little note box, with its natural, kraft paper finish,

I knew I had to paint something on it. The color of the paper lends itself so well

to reeds, and I thought a dragonfly would be the perfect addition.

Materials

- papier-mâché note box
- no. 1 liner brush
- no. 4 round stroke brush
- no. 6 filbert
- no. 10 shader brush
- ruler
- pencil
- stylus
- white transfer paper
- dragonfly pattern (page 25)

DecoArt Americana Acrylic Paints

- Celery Green
- Light Avocado
- Light Buttermilk
- Midnite Green
- Raw Umber
- Reindeer Moss Green
- Sable Brown

1 Freehand Reeds in Raw Umber

Using the dragonfly pattern and the white transfer paper, transfer the image onto the top center of the note box with a stylus. Using the no. 4 round stroke brush and Raw Umber, freehand the reeds, going through the wings, but avoiding the body of the dragonfly. Vary the pressure of the brush to create thick and thin reeds. Continue the lines of the reeds around the side and back of the box. A liner may be used if desired for some of the thinner reeds. Create a total of about seven reeds, varying in width.

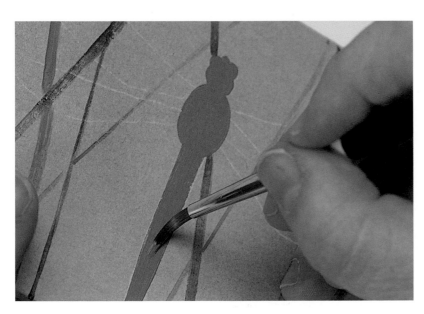

2 Add Reeds in Sable Brown

Add additional reeds with the no. 4 round stroke brush and Sable Brown. Do not cross through the wide Raw Umber reeds, stop and "go under" the reed to make it look like it is behind the darker reed. Create about three thin and one wide reed.

3 Basecoat Dragonfly Body

Using the no. 4 round stroke brush and Light Avocado, basecoat all of the dragonfly body, head, tail, eyes and nose. Leave the wings alone at this point.

4 Add the Shine Spot

Dampen the body with water, then add a shine line of Reindeer Moss Green using the liner brush. When adding a shine spot, I like to prepare by dampening the entire image that's getting the spot, so that the color can diffuse a little and not reach a dry spot. This will give your piece a soft look. Let the area dry and see if you need to do it again in the same spot.

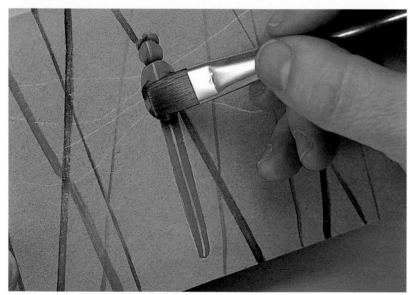

Tip

For a wider application of a shine spot, you can press your liner flat or use a round brush.

5 Shade the Dragonfly

Shade with Midnite Green and the no. 10 shader brush. Walk out the brush well first. Shade where the body connects to the tail and the head, the eyes and the nose. On the body, shade under each set of wings.

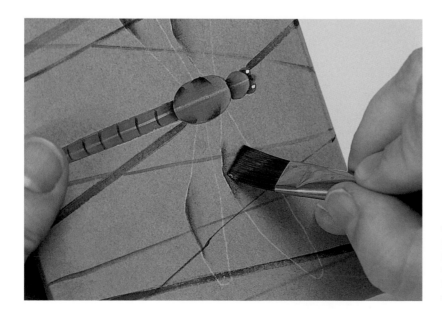

6 Segment the Tail

With the liner and Midnite Green, create the segment lines on the tail. Highlight the head, the body and the last four sections of the tail with Celery Green using the no. 10 shader. Dot they eyes with Light Buttermilk. Using the no. 10 shader and Raw Umber, add shade spots to the wings.

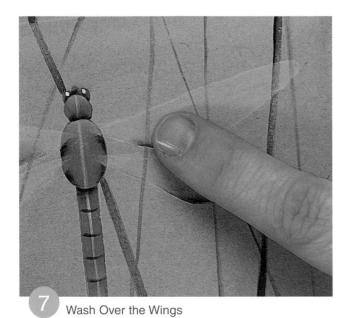

7 Wash Over the Wings

Load the no. 6 filbert with Reindeer Moss Green and enough water to make the color transparent. This is known as a wash. Brush this this color over the surface of all of the wings (the shade spots should still be visible.) Pull from the body out, beginning actually on the body. While wet, press your finger down on the concentrated areas and lift the paint over the dark spots.

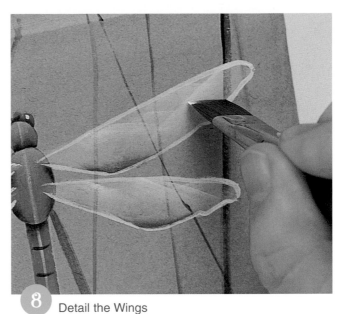

8 Detail the Wings

Outline the wings with a liner and Light Buttermilk. Start heavier on the outer edge and fade as you head toward the body. Where the wings are ruffled along the bottom, waver the brush. To add sparkle, slip-slap lightly with a side-loaded no. 10 shader and Light Buttermilk, avoiding the dark spots. Lightly erase any pattern lines. Sign your name, and apply sealant to finish (see tips on finishing, page 15).

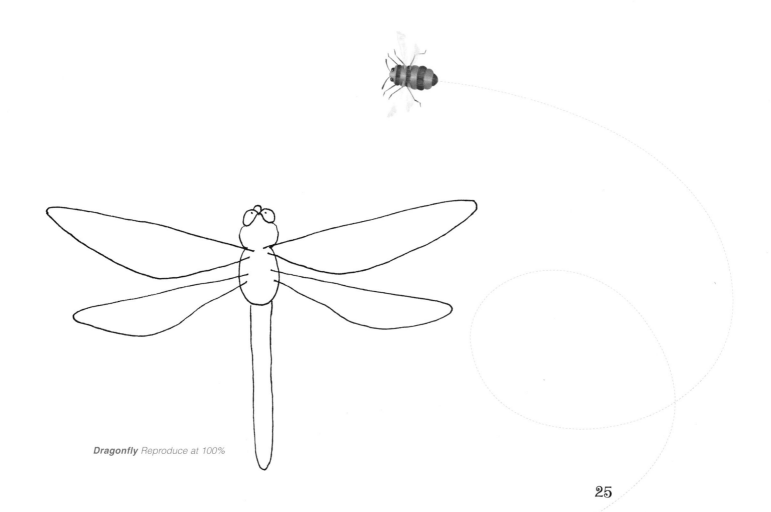

Dragonfly *Reproduce at 100%*

Let Me Call You "Beeheart"

This little heart can be put anywhere to remind you of someone special. The cute little bee cutout really pops from the surface, but if you don't wish to use one, use the pattern provided to transfer him right onto the basecoated heart surface.

Materials

- wooden heart plaque
- wooden bee cutout (optional)
- wood sealer
- no. 1 liner brush
- no. 4 round stroke brush
- no. 2 shader brush
- no. 8 shader brush
- no. 10 shader brush
- 1-inch (25mm) basecoater
- stencil sponge
- wood glue (optional)
- stylus
- white transfer paper
- chintz stencil
- bee pattern (page 29)

DecoArt Americana Acrylic Paints

Antique Gold	Rookwood Red
Burnt Sienna	Sand
Delane's Dark Flesh	Soft Black
Driftwood	

1 Stencil the Heart

Prepare the heart surface with sealer and Rookwood Red (see Preparing a Wood Surface, page 10). Stencil onto the top curves and the point at the bottom of the heart using a portion (tulips and leaves) of the chintz stencil with Delane's Dark Flesh and the stencil sponge. If needed after stenciling, you can sharpen or clean up the image using Rookwood Red and a liner brush.

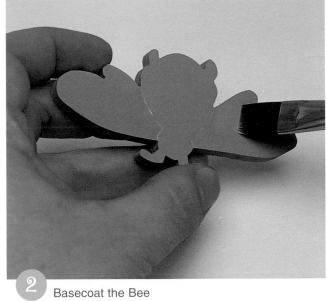

2 Basecoat the Bee

If you are not using a wooden cutout, transfer the bee pattern to the heart, using a stylus and white transfer paper. Paint a basecoat of Antique Gold over the entire surface of the bee on the heart or over the entire cutout. Sand the wooden bee lightly. Using a dampened no. 10 shader and Driftwood, apply a sheer coat onto the wing portions from the center out. Paint the wooden wing sides as well.

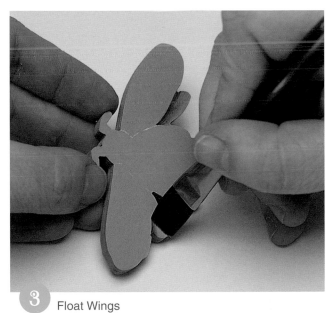

3 Float Wings

Using the transfer paper and a stylus, retrace the bee details. Using the no. 10 shader, separate the wings with a float of Soft Black.

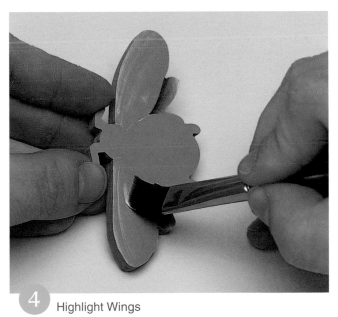

4 Highlight Wings

Using the no. 10 shader, highlight the wings with a float of Sand. Start at the body and work toward the outside, making several swipes to form vein lines. Highlight the bottom wing just on the outer tip.

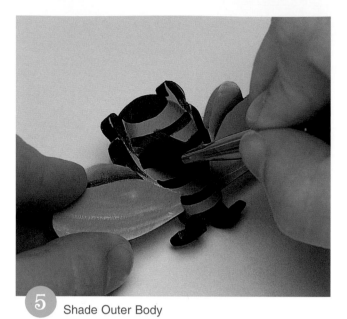

5 Shade Outer Body

Basecoat the antennae, dark body stripes and legs with Soft Black, using the no. 2 shader brush. Follow through onto the sides of the cutout. To make the body look rounded, shade the outer body edge with Burnt Sienna and the no. 10 shader brush.

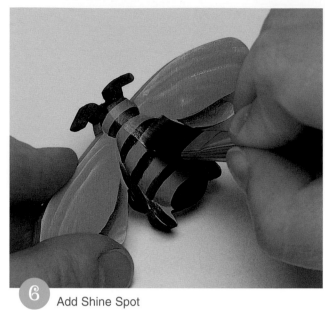

6 Add Shine Spot

Dampen the bee, then apply a shine spot of Sand down the center of the body using the liner brush. (For more information on this technique, see step 4 on page 24.)

7 Create Letter Boxes

Position the bee on the heart to check placement for the letter boxes. Using Driftwood and the no. 10 shader brush, make squares for letters. Start with the brush straight up and down on the chisel edge, pull straight down and lift the brush back up to the chisel edge before removing. Repeat for a total of four squares at the top for the "To Be." Don't worry if the paint goes on a bit sheer.

8 Add Letters and Finish

Repeat the process for the remaining squares using the no. 8 shader brush and Driftwood. Use the no. 4 round stroke brush to make the dots and a question mark. Then paint the letters with the same brush and Soft Black. To make letters, pull a line from right to left, then retrace from left to right to make all lines consistent. Turn the plaque as needed to keep strokes easy to form, such as those lines that are vertical. (See sidebar on page 29.) Glue the bee to the heart using wood glue. Sign your name, and apply sealant to finish (see tips on finishing, page 15).

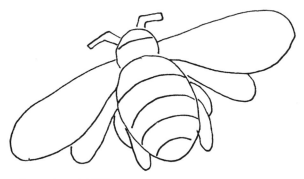

Bee *Reproduce pattern at 100%*

A Word on Hand Lettering

When lettering, the key to remember is consistency. Thin your paint just a bit with water and use the best liner or round brush you have. Pull from both ends of the letter so they are the same thickness on top and bottom. I like to flatten my brush tip so that the letters are nice and even, making them go together perfectly. Turn your surface as needed, so that all lines can be pulled horizontally.

Variation

Papier-mâché Ornament

1. Basecoat the entire ornament with Burnt Sienna. Basecoat the edges with Soft Black.
2. Using the no. 8 shader and Delane's Dark Flesh, apply the checked design. Start in the middle and work out from there.
3. Transfer the bee design over the checks with white transfer paper.
4. Follow steps 2–6 on pages 27 and 28 for the bee except separate the wings with a float of Burnt Sienna and highlight the feet and the antennae with Driftwood.
5. Create the motion swirl with Driftwood. Highlight with Sand, then shade with Burnt Sienna.

A Stitch to Share

The look of needlework on these coasters is mimicked so well everyone will be sure you stitched the

tags yourself! This boxed set makes a wonderful gift, and the coasters dress up any table.

Materials

- coaster set with box
- wood sealer
- no. 1 liner brush
- ¾-inch (19mm) wash brush
- 1-inch (25mm) basecoater
- sea sponge
- transparent tape
- craft knife
- ruler
- pencil
- stylus
- white transfer paper
- heart, flower and tag patterns (page 33)

DecoArt Americana Acrylic Paints

Antique White	Light Buttermilk
Burnt Sienna	Midnite Green
Driftwood	Mississippi Mud
French Mocha	Raw Umber
Light Avocado	

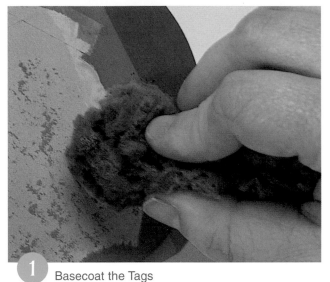

1 Basecoat the Tags

Prepare coasters and the coaster box with sealer and Mississippi Mud (see Preparing a Wood Surface, page 10). Using white transfer paper and a stylus, transfer one tag pattern onto each of the coasters. Transfer the lid pattern onto the lid. Tape off each tag using the transparent tape. Burnish down with your fingers to prevent any paint from seeping under it. On the lid, trim the tape where necessary with the craft knife. Basecoat tags with one coat of Antique White to neutralize the darkness of the Mississippi Mud. When dry, basecoat again with a coat of Driftwood. Mix two parts Driftwood to one part Midnite Green plus a touch of Mississippi Mud. Lightly sponge on this mixture with a dampened sea sponge.

2 Shade the Tags

Softly float a shade with a mixture of one part Driftwood and one part Raw Umber in a slip-slap manner using the ¾-inch (19mm) wash brush. Include the shading in at least three areas of the tag.

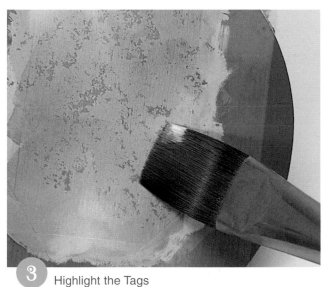

3 Highlight the Tags

Highlight with a mixture of one part Driftwood to three parts Light Buttermilk. Float softly in about three areas of the tag.

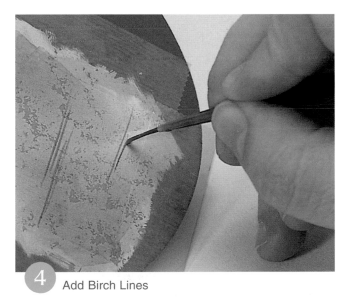

4 Add Birch Lines

Pull several horizontal lines with the liner and a mixture of one part Mississippi Mud to one part Raw Umber. These fine lines should be made with just the tip of the brush. Remove the tape from all the tags. If you need to clean up any edges, just use Mississippi Mud and the ¾-inch (19mm) wash brush.

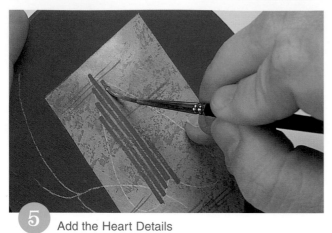

⑤ Add the Heart Details

Transfer the tag details. Fill in the tag holes with Mississippi Mud. Create the heart needlework on its particular coaster, using the liner brush with the tip pressed flat, ensuring consistent lines. Begin in the center of the heart with French Mocha. Pull one line straight in one direction, reload and, along the same line, begin at the opposite end and pull in that direction. This will ensure even pressure from start to finish so it will look like needlework.

⑥ Create the Tag String

Continue painting French Mocha lines, making about three lines on each side of the center. Then begin brush mixing in Burnt Sienna (see Brush Mixing, page 14) and continue to the outer edges of the heart. With the mixture that was used for the tag highlights (step 3) and the liner, create the tag string. Make sure the string goes behind the tag at some point and reappears at the tag hole. Add a ball for the knot in the string.

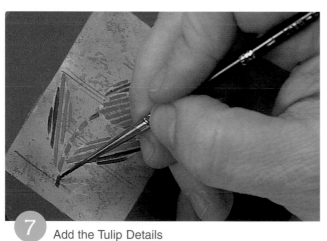

⑦ Add the Tulip Details

Transfer the tulip detail to its tag. Create the flower in the same manner as the heart, with French Mocha in the center, then mixing in Burnt Sienna toward the outside. Paint the leaves with three lines of Light Avocado on the top and two lines of Midnite Green on the bottom. Paint the grass lines with Midnite Green. Add the stem with a dashed line of Light Avocado. Pull Midnite Green on the top and bottom stitches. Add the string and knot with the mixture used before and the liner.

⑧ Add the Flower Details

Transfer the five-petal flower to its tag and create the petals with the liner and French Mocha. Add the center with a few short lines of Burnt Sienna. Pull stitches for the stem with the liner and Midnite Green, and create the leaves and grass with the liner and Light Avocado. Add the string and knot with the mixture used in step 6.

⑨ Create Lid Details

For the lid, transfer the heart and flower details and then fill in as instructed in step 5. Basecoat the ladybug body with Burnt Sienna, using the liner. Add the head, legs, antennae and spot with Midnite Green. Highlight the body with French Mocha and the ¾-inch (19mm) wash brush. Separate the two tags with a soft float of Raw Umber. Sign your name, and apply sealant to finish (see tips on finishing, page 15).

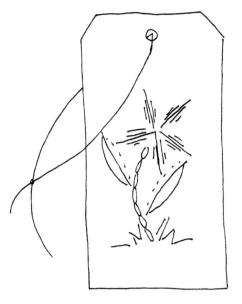

Flower *Enlarge pattern at 111%*

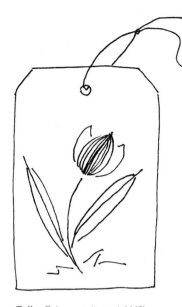

Tulip *Enlarge pattern at 111%*

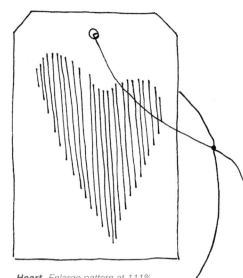

Heart *Enlarge pattern at 111%*

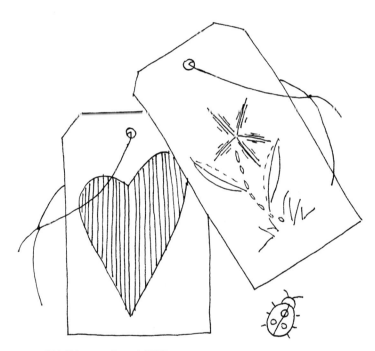

Lid *Enlarge pattern at 120%*

Tip

For added protection, apply a thin coat of paste wax to each coaster to prevent water damage. If you run it along the inside of the box lid, it will also prevent sticking.

Dotted Dinnerware

I am in love with polka dots of any size, so I decided to add a little pizzazz

to the lovely flowers on this simple plate. Aren't they charming? When complete,

this piece can be displayed on a plate easel or propped up on a mantle.

Materials

- 9½" (24cm) wooden plate
- wood sealer
- no. 1 liner brush
- no. 1 script liner
- no. 6 filbert brush
- no. 8 flat brush
- ¾-inch (19mm) wash brush

- 1-inch (25mm) basecoater
- stencil sponge
- stylus
- white transfer paper
- white charcoal pencil
- polka dot stencil
- flower pattern (page 37)

DecoArt Americana Acrylic Paints

Celery Green	Mocha
Delane's Dark Flesh	Raw Umber
Driftwood	Soft Peach
Mississippi Mud	

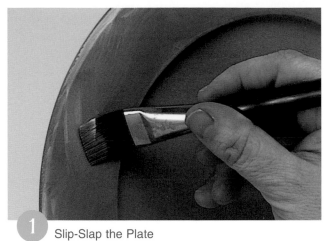

1 Slip-Slap the Plate

Prepare the plate with sealer and Mississippi Mud (see Preparing a Wood Surface, page 10). When dry, sand and apply a second coat of Mississippi Mud. While the second coat is still wet, slip-slap Driftwood from the outer edge inward, using the 1-inch (25mm) basecoater. Let your strokes show. Do the slip-slap on the rim only. Let dry.

2 Stencil on the Dots

Using the stencil sponge, the polka dot stencil and Celery Green, apply dots to the plate interior. The circles closest to the rim will require extra pressure to ensure polka dot coverage. Reload sponge as needed. Clean up any dots with Mississippi Mud and the liner brush.

3 Create the Flower

Transfer the flower pattern onto the plate center, using white transfer paper and the stylus. Using the no. 8 flat brush, basecoat the center of the flower with Delane's Dark Flesh, and the petals with Mocha. Two coats for each are more than sufficient. Using the ¾-inch (19mm) wash brush and Raw Umber, shade the top of the inside circle as well as the outside of the flower center. This will begin to form a button.

4 Make the Button Rim

Using the ¾-inch (19mm) wash brush and Mocha, highlight to form an inside rim of the button. Let dry.

5 Add the Button Holes and Thread

Using the stylus, add four dots to the center of the button using Mississippi Mud, and let dry. Erase any remaining graphite lines. Using the liner and Driftwood, create an "X" for the string of the button, curving the lines slightly.

35

6 Shade the Petals

Using the ¾-inch (19mm) wash brush, shade the flower petals using Delane's Dark Flesh. Create shading that is about ½" (1cm) wide and is near the center.

7 Highlight the Petals

Highlight the points of each petal about ½" (1cm) down with Soft Peach, using the ¾-inch (19mm) wash brush.

8 Add the Veining

Using the same brush, load for a float with Delane's Dark Flesh. Use the chisel end to make the veining on one side of each petal. The veining is done by laying the chisel edge down, then pulling up the flower petal in short, rapid motions. Repeat on the opposite side of each petal with a float of Soft Peach.

9 Outline the Petal

Thin Driftwood with a bit of water for nice consistent linework. Using the script liner with soft, even pressure, begin near the flower center and pull a line out toward the tip. Repeat on the opposite side of each petal and continue outlining until each one is complete.

10 Highlight the Petal Tips

To highlight the petal tips, place the Driftwood-loaded brush into Soft Peach. Start at the outer petal point and pull toward the flower's center, letting the stroke fade naturally.

11 Add Rim Flowers

Around the rim of the plate, using the white charcoal pencil, make a mark at each point that is centered in between the petals of the large, center flower. Then dot with Delane's Dark Flesh for the freehand flower centers. Pull the petals using the no. 6 filbert brush and Mocha. Start with a firm pressure on the brush, then release at a slight curve. Pull from the outside into the flower center. (If you don't wish to freehand the flowers, or the tendrils that follow, transfer them from the pattern provided below.)

12 Add Tendrils

Outline the center of each rim flower with Raw Umber and the liner brush. Add a Driftwood dot to each center with the liner. Create leaves and tendrils with Celery Green. Paint the leaves with the filbert brush, just like the small rim flower petals, only pull from the flower out. Add the tendrils with the liner brush.

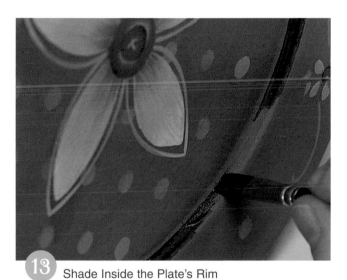

13 Shade Inside the Plate's Rim

Using Celery Green and the polka dot stencil, sponge one dot in between each of the flowers on the rim. Use the no. 8 flat brush and Raw Umber for the inner edge of the plate. Sign your name, and apply sealant to finish (see tips on finishing, page 15).

Flower and Tendrils Enlarge at 125%

37

"Tote"ally Sweet

When I found this charming tote box, I knew the subject would have to be just as sweet.

The vines, berries and cute little leaves of bittersweet were just the ticket. This tote could have

many uses, including napkin storage, holding guest soaps, or even holding cherished letters.

Materials

- small wooden tote
- wood sealer
- no. 4 round stroke brush
- ¾-inch (19mm) wash brush
- 1-inch (25mm) basecoater
- pencil
- stylus
- white transfer paper
- branch pattern (page 39)

DecoArt Americana Acrylic Paints

Antique Gold	Midnite Green
Antique White	Mississippi Mudd
Delane's Dark Flesh	Raw Umber
French Mocha	Tomato Red

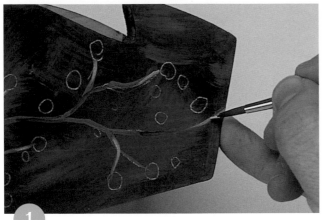

1 Transfer the Branch Pattern

Prepare the outside of the tote with sealer and Midnite Green (see Preparing a Wood Surface, page 10). Apply a wash of sealer and Mississippi Mud to the inside of the tote and the handle, using the 1-inch (25mm) basecoater. Sand and basecoat the outside again with Midnite Green. While the paint is still wet, slip-slap in Mississippi Mud with the ¾-inch (19mm) wash brush. Sand lightly. Transfer the branch pattern to the tote with the white transfer paper. For the short sides of the tote, use a portion of the pattern, lining it up with a branch on the long side. Using the no. 4 round stroke brush and Mississippi Mud, stroke on the branches, varying the pressure. Bittersweet branches are more angular than curved. Add highlights here and there with Antique White, and shade with Raw Umber.

2 Paint in the Berries

Basecoat the berries with the no. 4 round brush and one coat of Delane's Dark Flesh. Shade the berries with a float of Tomato Red in the area closest to the stem, using the ¾-inch (19mm) wash brush. This does not require too much precision; the effect will be subtle. Highlight the top sides of the berries with French Mocha, walking the brush out well first.

3 Add the Leaves to Finish

Create the leaves with the no. 4 round brush and alternate between Antique Gold and Antique White, keeping all the leaves on one berry the same color. Start each leaf at the stem end near the berry and pull outward. There should be no more than three leaves per berry and all of the berries should have at least one leaf. Sign your name, and apply sealant to finish (see tips on finishing, page 15).

Branch *Enlarge at 135%*

39

Buzzin' Box

I love to play games and I love clever ways to store them even more.

Who says bees aren't welcome at a friendly game of cards?

The polka dots on this project make the end result all the more endearing.

Materials

- wooden double-deck card box
- wood sealer
- no. 1 liner brush
- no. 1 script liner
- no. 6 filbert brush
- no. 10 shader brush
- ¾-inch (19mm) wash brush
- 1-inch (25mm) basecoater
- stencil sponge
- ¾-inch (19mm) transparent tape
- pencil
- stylus
- white transfer paper
- polka dot stencil
- bee pattern (page 43)

DecoArt Americana Acrylic Paints

Antique Gold	Raw Umber
Celery Green	Reindeer Moss Green
Light Avocado	Sand
Midnite Green	

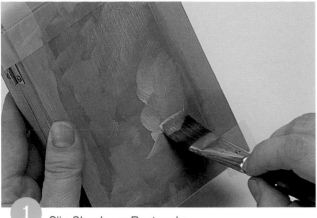

1 Slip-Slap Inner Rectangle

Prepare card box with sealer and Light Avocado (see Preparing a Wood Surface, page 10). Tape off the lid using ¾" (19mm) tape. Burnish well with your finger. Base the inner rectangle again using the ¾-inch (19mm) wash brush and Light Avocado. While wet, slip-slap with a corner-loaded brush of Celery Green, then Reindeer Moss Green. Let dry.

2 Shade With Midnite Green

Using the ¾-inch (19mm) wash brush, float a shade of Midnite Green around the inside of the rectangle edge, along the tape. Pull from one side to the other.

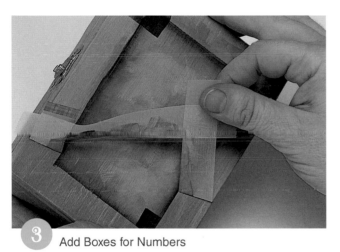

3 Add Boxes for Numbers

Using the no. 10 shader brush, create two boxes in two opposite corners with Midnite Green. Make the boxes the width of the brush and about ¾" (19mm) long. Remove the tape.

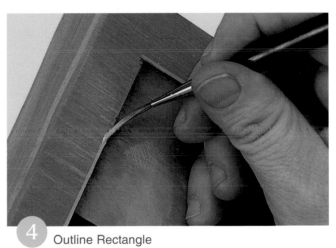

4 Outline Rectangle

Using a bit of water mixed with Celery Green and the no. 1 script liner, pull a fine line around the perimeter of the shaded area. A script liner works best for going long distances because it holds more paint.

5 Add Numbers

Using the script liner and Reindeer Moss Green, highlight the line on the outer two corners where the two boxes are. Using Celery Green and the regular liner, paint the number 2 inside each of the boxes.

Tip

When using tape as a mask, start painting with your brush on top of the tape and work your strokes inward.

41

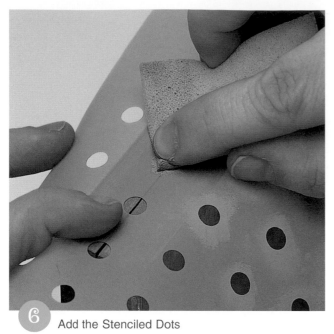

6 Add the Stenciled Dots

Center four dots from the polka dot stencil along one long side on the top of the box. Using the sponge and Celery Green, stencil in the dots. Repeat on the opposite long side. Center one dot between the corner dots on each of the short sides. Let the dots dry, then stencil in three rows of four dots on the box bottom. Along the front side of the box, center one dot on either side of the clasp in the front of the box (half of a dot on the lid, and half on the box bottom) and one dot between the hinges in the back. Center two dots on each short side.

7 Add the Bee

Transfer the bee pattern to the center of the lid, using the white transfer paper and a stylus. Trace only the outline of the bees. Basecoat the bees with the no. 10 shader and Antique Gold. Add the eyes, legs and antennae with Raw Umber and the liner brush.

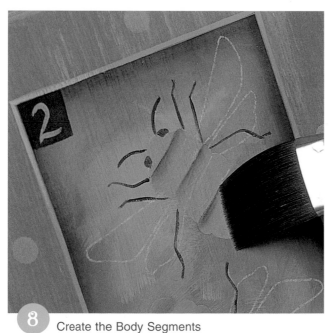

8 Create the Body Segments

Float Raw Umber horizontally with the ¾-inch (19mm) wash brush, creating four sections on each bee body.

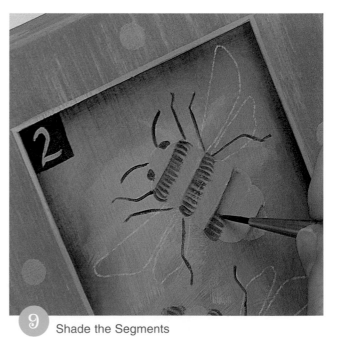

9 Shade the Segments

Using the regular liner and Raw Umber, softly shade each dark section by pulling vertical lines from the top, down.

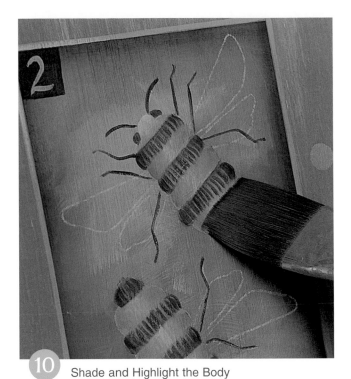

10 Shade and Highlight the Body

Using the ¾-inch (19mm) wash brush, float the outer edges of each dark section with Raw Umber. Highlight the yellow sections of the bodies with a brush mix of Antique Gold and a touch of Sand. Shade these same sections with a brush mix of Antique Gold and a touch of Raw Umber.

11 Create the Bee's Wings

To create the wings, use a wash of Sand and the no. 6 filbert. Pull strokes from the outside of the wings into the body, going right over the legs.

12 Float Sand on the Wings

Using the ¾-inch (19mm) wash brush, float the outer tips with Sand to brighten if needed. Highlight eyes with a dot of Sand, using the liner. Float Light Avocado lightly to separate wings. Sign your name, and apply sealant to finish (see tips on finishing, page 15).

> ## Tip
>
> When basecoating an individual element that has been transferred from a pattern, begin a little in from the line, and then push the paint outward to meet the line.

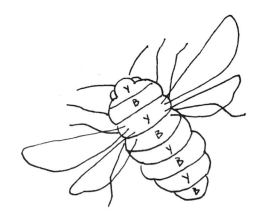

Bee *Reproduce at 100%*

ADD WATER *and* SUNLIGHT

Now is the time to nurture all of those new ideas in your head and add a few sprinklings of texture.

The addition of a richly surfaced background is something I want to share with you in this section. Compressed sponges can be cut into any shape or size, giving you the opportunity to use them to create texture in your background or to add an artistic element in the composition. A sea sponge is a great tool that can't be beat for its irregular and natural pattern, and don't throw out that toothbrush that's worn—its promise of spectacular spatter adds sparkle and depth to the surface of your project.

Spring has sprung—let's watch your skills blossom and grow while you create new beauty you can truly take pride in!

Diamond Dinnerware

When I received this little tin cup, I knew it deserved something larger than life.
My solution, a huge, oversized ladybug. I love patterns, so I created diamonds to complement
the hobnail plate design. I thought including a butterfly was a great addition.

Materials

- small tin cup, primed
- hobnail tin plate, primed
- no. 1 liner brush
- no. 8 flat brush
- ¾-inch (19mm) wash brush
- compressed sponge
- sea sponge
- scissors
- ruler
- pencil
- stylus
- white transfer paper
- white charcoal pencil
- ladybug pattern (page 51)
- butterfly pattern (page 51)

DecoArt Americana Acrylic Paints

- Antique Gold
- Antique White
- Delane's Dark Flesh
- French Mocha
- Rookwood Red
- Soft Black
- Tomato Red

Ladybug Cup

1 Sponge on Rookwood Red

Before starting, see Basic Tinware Prep on page 51. Using Soft Black and a dampened sea sponge, pounce paint over the entire outside of the cup, letting some of the original primer show through. Let dry. Using a pencil and ruler, create a 2" × 2" (5cm × 5cm) square on the compressed sponge. Cut out the square with scissors. Wet the sponge to expand, and wring dry. Completely dip one square side into Rookwood Red and pounce excess paint off onto the palette. Begin the first stamp on the cup near the handle with the square oriented as a diamond shape. Rock the sponge from one side to the other. Begin the second and third diamonds with the tips touching to complete a diamond-row pattern.

2 Basecoat the Ladybug

After sponging the cup, let dry. Using your liner, add a dot to the connecting points in the back of the cup with a basecoat of Tomato Red and the liner brush. Add a highlight of French Mocha to the dot. Transfer the ladybug pattern to the front of the cup, centering it over the two connecting points with the white transfer paper and a stylus. Basecoat the wings with the no. 8 flat brush and Tomato Red. Basecoat the light sections of the face and head with Antique White and the dark sections of the face with Soft Black. With the liner, apply the legs and antennae with French Mocha.

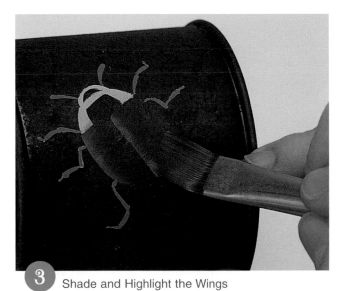

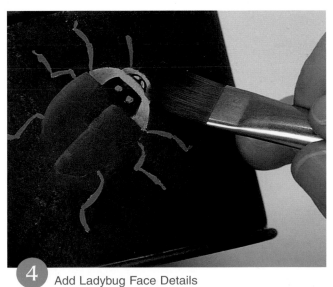

3 Shade and Highlight the Wings

Add spots to the wings with Soft Black and the liner. Shade the wings with a float of Rookwood Red and a touch of Soft Black, using the ¾-inch (19mm) wash brush. Highlight the wings with French Mocha, going right over the top of the spots.

4 Add Ladybug Face Details

Create the top two spots on the face with Antique White, and the bottom two spots with a brush mix of Antique White plus French Mocha. Shade the light outer section of the head and face with French Mocha and the ¾-inch (19mm) wash brush. Sign your name, and apply sealant to finish (see tips on finishing, page 15).

47

Butterfly Plate

1 Trace the Plate

See Basic Tinware Prep on page 51. Using a dampened sea sponge, sponge Soft Black over the entire surface of the front of the plate. Frequently rotate your sponge to prevent making a noticeable pattern. Let the paint dry completely. Tape together enough tracing paper to cover the plate. Set the plate upside down on the tracing paper and trace the outline. Set the plate aside. Fold the circle shape in half, then fold in half again in the same direction.

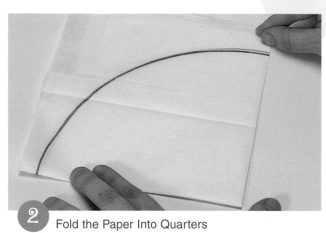

2 Fold the Paper Into Quarters

Unfold this second fold and with the paper still folded in half once, fold into the opposite direction. The shape will be a quarter of a circle.

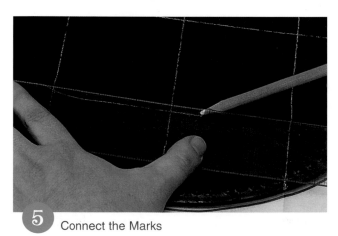

3 Fold in Half Again

Fold this in half again in the same direction. Unfold the paper.

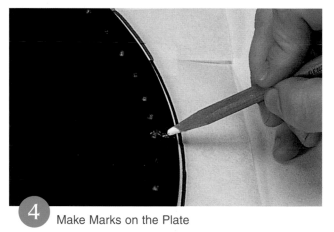

4 Make Marks on the Plate

Place the plate right side up over the circle on the paper. With the white charcoal pencil, make marks around the perimeter of the plate wherever there is a fold mark on the tracing paper.

5 Connect the Marks

Using the ruler and the white charcoal pencil, lightly connect all these marks to form a grid.

6 Create Square Sponge

Using a ruler and pencil, draw a 2" × 2" (5cm × 5cm) square onto the compressed sponge. Using the scissors, cut out the square. Wet the sponge to expand, and wring dry. The points of the sponge will meet the lines on the plate grid, with the center being over the intersecting points.

7 Stamp Onto the Plate

Dip the compressed sponge into Rookwood Red and pounce off excess paint onto the palette. Begin stamping with the sponge in the center of the plate and work your way out to the perimeter. When reaching the rim of the plate, press the sponge into the rim from the inside out.

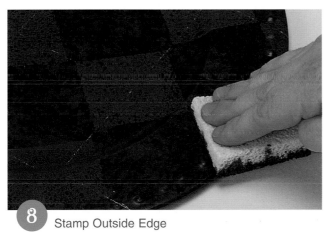

8 Stamp Outside Edge

For the outside edge of the rim, press firmly to work paint in and around the raised hobnail beading. A clean, damp sponge can clean up any paint in areas that may need it.

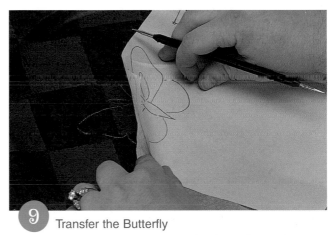

9 Transfer the Butterfly

When dry, use a damp brush to remove the charcoal pencil lines. Don't apply any pressure because it can remove the sponged-on paint. Using the pattern on page 51, transfer the butterfly to the center of the plate with white transfer paper and a stylus.

Tip

When applying paint with a sponge, if the sponged-on paint is raised too high in spots after it has dried, sand it lightly with a paper bag to smooth it down a bit.

10 Basecoat the Butterfly

Base the butterfly body with Soft Black and the no. 1 liner. Base the wings with Delane's Dark Flesh and the ¾-inch (19mm) wash brush. The wings may require three coats.

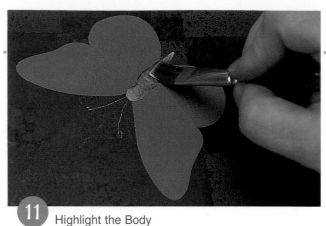

11 Highlight the Body

Using the ¾-inch (19mm) wash brush, highlight the body with Antique White. Highlight the tip of the tail, then begin at the top of the head and walk the brush down the length of the body. Wash Delane's Dark Flesh over the body to tone down the white.

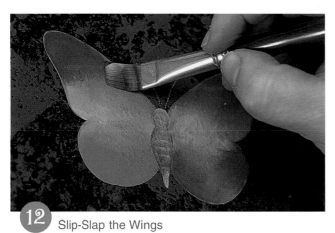

12 Slip-Slap the Wings

With Delane's Dark Flesh, basecoat each wing again. While wet, slip-slap Antique Gold near the bottom of the top wing with the ¾ inch (19mm) wash brush. Slip slap Rookwood Red around the top outer edges of the top wings and near the body on the lower wings. Minimize the brushstrokes so that the look is smooth.

13 Shade the Wings

Load Soft Black onto the ¾-inch (19mm) wash brush as you would for a float. Using the chisel edge, move the brush back and forth horizontally about ¼" (6mm) around the perimeter of the wings, following their curves. Stay up on the chisel edge for nice straight lines. This gives the wings a ruffled look.

14 Add the Wing Details

Softly shade with Rookwood Red and the ¾-inch (19mm) wash brush under the top wings. Add in the wing details with the liner and Antique White. Start with the "eye" shapes, then make the lines. Add in the dots, then the antennae. Sign your name, and apply sealant to finish (see tips on finishing, page 15).

Tip

When painting on metal surfaces, a fairly dry brush works best. If the paint starts to lift off the surface, heat set it with a blow dryer before continuing.

Ladybug *Reproduce at 100%*

Basic Tinware Prep

The tinware I used in this book comes primed and ready to paint. If you find an area that has been scratched or is dented, lightly sand with fine sandpaper, then apply DecoArt's Multi-Purpose Sealer to the area and beyond. Let it dry, then basecoat with Asphaltum (this color matches the primer). Proceed with the rest of the instructions.

If using tinware that you found at a tag sale, clean it with soap and water, then let it dry completely. You can buy a primer at your local hardware store or you can apply a coat of Multi-Purpose Sealer and then basecoat with the color of choice.

When finishing tinware, I always let it cure for at least 24 hours before varnishing. If you are in an area of high humidity, I would let it sit for at least 3 days before varnishing.

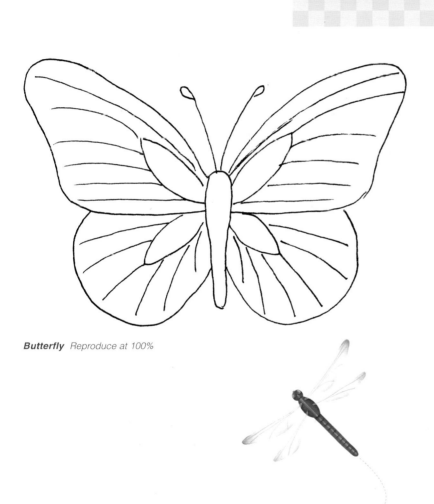

Butterfly *Reproduce at 100%*

Shades of Green Box

I love including texture on projects, and adding these sponged-on leaves satisfies that need just fine. Besides, it is so fitting for the little ladybug subjects. Don't you think?

Materials

- wooden triangle box
- wooden balls for feet (3)
- wood sealer
- no. 1 liner brush
- no. 8 shader brush
- ¾-inch (19mm) wash brush
- 1-inch (25mm) basecoater
- compressed sponge
- scissors
- stylus
- graphite paper
- white transfer paper
- wood glue
- leaf and ladybug patterns (page 55)

DecoArt Americana Acrylic Paints

- Antique Gold
- Forest Green
- Midnite Green
- Mistletoe
- Payne's Grey
- Titanium White
- Tomato Red

1 Basecoat the Box

Prepare the entire box with sealer and Forest Green (see Preparing a Wood Surface, page 10).

2 Paint the Ball Feet

Paint the ball knob feet with a basecoat of sealer and Midnite Green.

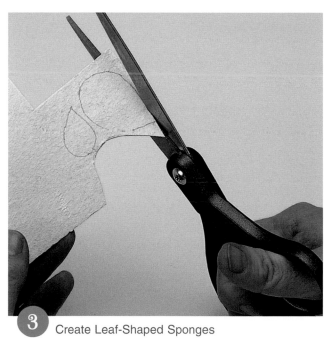

3 Create Leaf-Shaped Sponges

Using the leaf pattern, transfer leaf shapes onto the compressed sponge using graphite paper and a stylus. Cut out the shapes with scissors. Immerse the leaf shapes into water to expand, then wring out.

4 Load a Leaf With Midnite Green

Mix two parts of Forest Green with one part of Midnite Green and using the largest leaf shape, load the paint onto the sponge. Make sure to get the whole shape into the paint. Pounce the leaf onto the palette to remove the excess paint.

Tip

When basecoating a long area, use fewer long strokes, rather than more short strokes. This will aid the look of a float, if used, later on.

⑤ Stamp the Large Leaves

On each side of the box, including the top, stamp four or five large leaves. Press down onto the sponge firmly, but do not flatten. Wrap the sponge around the edges when necessary. This is the most subtle layer of leaves, so don't worry about it not really popping out. Rinse the sponge in water and wring dry.

⑥ Add the Other Leaves and Stems

Using Midnite Green and the smallest leaf, repeat step 5, adding five to seven leaves on each side. Place a few of these small leaves together to look as if they are joined. Mix two parts Mistletoe to one part Forest Green and, using the middle leaf size and this mixture, stamp three to four leaves on each side. Using the Midnite Green and the Mistletoe-Forest Green mixture and the liner brush, add stems to each of the small and medium leaves. Pull from the bottom of the stem up to, but not into, the leaf. Lightly sand any areas where the paint is raised.

⑦ Transfer the Ladybugs

Using white transfer paper, a stylus and the ladybug pattern, add one ladybug to each side of the box, wherever you wish to place them.

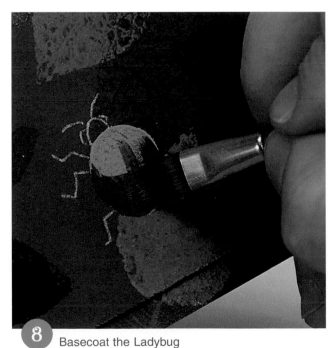

⑧ Basecoat the Ladybug

Using the no. 8 shader, basecoat the ladybug wings with Antique Gold. This will neutralize the green and allow the red that will go on next to be brighter. After this is dry, basecoat over the gold with Tomato Red.

⑨ Brush Blend Red and White

Brush blend the Tomato Red and Titanium White by sideloading a bit of red, then just dip into the white. Press down a few times onto the palette paper to mix slightly. The paint should be combined well so that you do not see two distinct colors.

⑩ Finish Ladybug and Add the Box Feet

With this brush mix and the ¾-inch (19mm) wash brush, float on highlights to the top of each individual wing. Make a brush blend of Payne's Grey and Tomato Red, and apply a shade to the under side of each wing. Using Payne's Grey and the liner, add the head, legs and one spot to each wing. Highlight the antennae and legs with Payne's Grey and a touch of Titanium White. Then, using the ¾-inch (19mm) wash brush and a brush blend of these two colors, highlight the head and spots. Glue the ball feet to the box bottom using wood glue. Sign your name, and apply sealant to finish (see tips on finishing, page 15).

Leaf Reproduce at 100%

Ladybug Reproduce at 100%

Beachcomber Basket

I love picking up seashells by the shore and thought this basket

would be perfect for holding such little treasures.

Materials

- small wooden-top basket
- wood sealer
- no. 1 liner brush
- ⅜-inch (10mm) DM Stippler brush
- ¾-inch (19mm) wash brush
- 1-inch (25mm) basecoater
- sea sponge
- old toothbrush
- pencil
- stylus
- super chacopaper
- shell basket pattern (page 61)

DecoArt Americana Acrylic Paints

	Antique White		Light Buttermilk
	Burnt Sienna		Mocha
	Driftwood		Sable Brown

1 Basecoat Basket and Add Shell

Prepare the basket lid (including the leather hinge) with sealer and Mocha (see Preparing a Wood Surface, page 10). Basecoat the lid's edge and underside with wood sealer and Driftwood. Let this dry, then sand and basecoat again with just the color. Dampen and wring out the sea sponge. Dip into Driftwood, pounce out excess paint onto the palette. Pounce onto the lid only. Using the toothbrush, spatter separately with Driftwood, Sable Brown and Light Buttermilk. Transfer the shell design using a stylus and super chacopaper. Basecoat the shell with Antique White and the ¾-inch (19mm) wash brush. On the left side of the shell, make small U-shaped strokes to create texture with Sable Brown and the ¾-inch (19mm) wash brush. On the right side, float Sable Brown in long, sweeping strokes from right to left. Deepen these strokes with Burnt Sienna.

2 Highlight the Shell

Highlight with Light Buttermilk, again making U-strokes, but in the opposite direction. Highlight the long, sweeping strokes as well with Light Buttermilk. Using the liner and Sable Brown, add a few horizontal fine lines to show the long contour of the shell.

3 Add Small Stones in the Sand

Create a shadow in the sand by stippling in Sable Brown with the DM Stippler. Pounce most of the paint off onto a paper towel first, so that the color is very soft. Add little stones with Sable Brown and the liner. Shade the left side of the stones with Burnt Sienna. Add some smaller stones with Light Buttermilk.

4 Create the Water

To create the water, wash in Light Buttermilk using the ¾-inch (19mm) wash brush. Pull in a horizontal direction, keeping all the strokes in one direction, like the tide. Let dry, then using the DM Stippler, stipple in Light Buttermilk to form the foam on the water.

5 Add Shadow to the Water

Using the ¾-inch (19mm) wash brush, float Burnt Sienna from the basket edge in horizontal strokes to add a shadow to the water. Shade where the water meets the sand to the right of the shell with Driftwood, using the ¾-inch (19mm) wash brush. Remove any super chacopaper lines with a damp brush. Sign your name, and apply sealant to finish (see tips on finishing, page 15).

Shell of a Time

Tags and clocks are so hot in home décor right now that I wanted to combine the two together and include a touch of the sea. I hope you'll love the results as much as I do.

Materials

- small wooden clock, including clock movements
- wood sealer
- no. 1 liner brush
- no. 4 flat brush
- ¾-inch (19mm) wash brush
- 1-inch (25mm) basecoater
- sea sponge
- old toothbrush
- transparent tape
- charcoal pencil
- stylus
- super chacopaper
- shell clock pattern (page 61)

DecoArt Americana Acrylic Paints

	Antique White		Sable Brown
	Driftwood		Sand
	Light Buttermilk		Soft Peach
	Mocha		

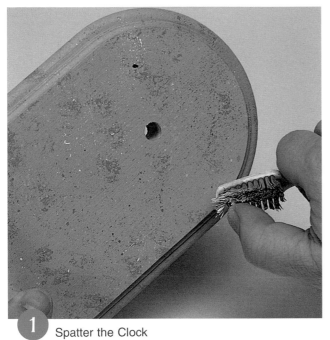

1 Spatter the Clock

Prepare entire clock with sealer and Mocha (see Preparing a Wood Surface, page 10). Dampen and wring out the sea sponge, then dip into Driftwood. Pounce out excess paint, then pounce paint onto clock, including the edges. Using the toothbrush, spatter with Driftwood, Sable Brown, Soft Peach and then Light Buttermilk. Try to apply an equal amount of each color.

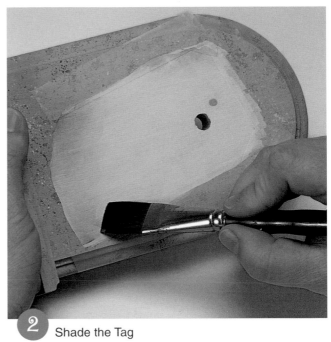

2 Shade the Tag

Using the stylus and the super chacopaper, transfer the tag portion of the pattern to the clock. Tape off the top and sides of the tag. Basecoat the tag with two coats of Sand, avoiding the hole at the top of the tag. Shade the tag with a float of Sable Brown and the ¾-inch (19mm) wash brush. This shading should be fairly mottled and not too straight.

3 Basecoat the Shell

Highlight the top right corner of the tag with Light Buttermilk and the ¾-inch (19mm) wash brush. Remove the tape and let dry. Transfer the shell pattern to the clock with super chacopaper and a stylus. Basecoat the area of the shell that sticks out over the end of the tag using the ¾-inch wash brush and Sand. When dry, basecoat the entire shell with Antique White and the ¾-inch (19mm) wash brush. For the ridged edge of the shell, wiggle the brush, rather than trying too hard to stay in the lines. Let the shell dry.

4 Create the Shell's Ridges

Continue using the ¾-inch (19mm) wash brush for all of the following steps here. Slip-slap the shell with Mocha. Shade with Sable Brown to separate the shell feet. With a brush mix of Sable Brown plus Mocha, stipple from the feet area upward about halfway to create the shell's ridges, staying up on the chisel end of the brush.

5 Add More Stippling

From the top down, repeat the stippling process, but with Driftwood. Then highlight with Light Buttermilk, stippling in between the Driftwood lines.

6 Create the Shell Arcs

Use a charcoal pencil to draw the horizontal arcs on the shell. Using the no. 4 flat brush and Soft Peach, pounce in these arcs. Begin in the center of the shell and pounce out and downward, following the curved shape of the shell, so the paint is more concentrated in the center and thinner on the outside. Reload, and begin in the center again and pounce in the opposite direction.

7 Shade Under the Arcs

With Sable Brown and the ¾-inch (19mm) wash brush, shade down the sides of the shell lightly, avoiding the peach stripes. Also shade along under the peach bands with a wiggly motion to enhance the ridges.

8 Create the Hole Reinforcer

If you didn't leave the tag hole, fill it in with Mocha. Next to the hole, highlight all the way around with Light Buttermilk and the ¾-inch (19mm) wash brush. Create the hole reinforcer with Sable Brown. Try to keep the circular shape regular. On the right side, where the shell meets the tag, shade with Sable Brown also, to create the weight of the tag.

9 Add the String

Pull a thin line for the string, using the liner and Sable Brown. With the ¾-inch (19mm) wash brush and Sable Brown, shade along the sand line, giving it a nice deep shadow. At this time, add any additional shading to the tag that you may think is needed.

10 Add the Pebbles

Highlight the sand with Soft Peach and the ¾-inch (19mm) wash brush. Add fairly transparent Sable Brown pebbles that vary in size, with the liner. Create additional pebbles with Light Buttermilk. Shade the Sable Brown pebbles with the ¾-inch (19mm) wash brush and a wash of Sable Brown. Sign your name, and apply sealant to finish (see tips on finishing, page 15). Follow the manufacturer's directions to add the clock movements.

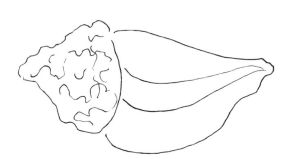

Shell Basket Enlarge at 125%

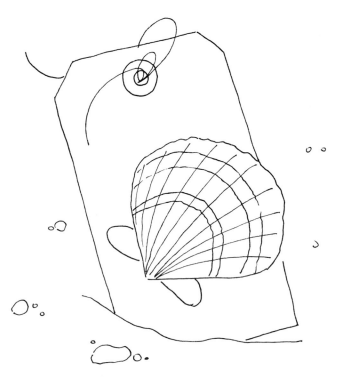

Shell Clock Enlarge at 125%

Nest Essentials

For texture on this box, I wanted something different yet easy to achieve.

Sponging above and below the stripe fit the bill perfectly.

Fill the box with bath essentials and give it as a gift. It is sure to please!

Materials

- wooden square box
- wooden half-egg
- wood sealer
- no. 4 round stroke brush
- no. 6 filbert brush
- ¾-inch (19mm) wash brush
- 1-inch (25mm) basecoater
- old toothbrush
- sea sponge
- industrial adhesive
- ruler
- white charcoal pencil
- T-square
- pencil
- stylus
- super chacopaper
- ¾" (19mm) transparent tape
- egg and twig patterns (page 65)

DecoArt Americana Acrylic Paints

- Antique White
- Burnt Sienna
- Celery Green
- Light Avocado
- Light Buttermilk
- Reindeer Moss Green
- Sable Brown

① Sponge With Reindeer Moss Green

Prepare the box with sealer and Celery Green (see Preparing a Wood Surface, page 10). Measure 1" (3cm) from the bottom and mark with white charcoal pencil. Use a T-square to draw a horizontal line around the box at this mark. Place a line of tape around the box above this line, and burnish. Dip a sea sponge into water and wring it out. Dip the sponge into a puddle of Reindeer Moss Green, and pounce excess paint off onto the palette. Begin pouncing the paint over the surface of the box above the taped line. Rotate the sponge as you pounce to avoid getting a repeating pattern. Sponge the knob also.

② Sponge With Light Avocado

Using the same technique, sponge below the line with Light Avocado. Next to the top of the tape line, float a line of Reindeer Moss Green with the ¾-inch (19mm) wash brush. Float Light Avocado in a line at the bottom of the tape. Remove the tape.

③ Shade the Eggs

Transfer the egg/twig pattern to the sides of the box, and the twig pattern to the top of the box, using the super chacopaper and the stylus. Using the ¾-inch (19mm) wash brush, basecoat the transferred eggs on the box and the separate half-egg cutout with Antique White. Using the ¾-inch (19mm) wash brush and Sable Brown, shade the two eggs on the box from the back of the box toward the front. Shade the bottom of the half-egg cutout.

4 Push the Paint

Push the paint out toward the edge for a softer line. This is an easier way to control the paint. If you see the paint begin to go outside of the shape, simply pull back.

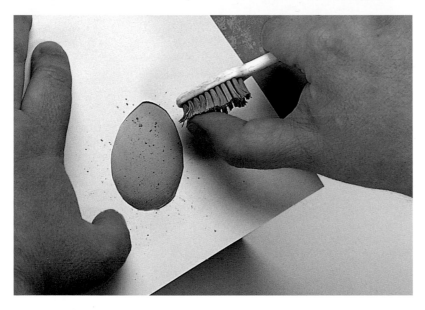

5 Spatter the Eggs

Highlight the eggs with Light Buttermilk and the ¾-inch (19mm) wash brush, placing the highlight opposite the shade. Highlight the top of the half-egg. Deepen the floated shade of the eggs with a very light amount of Burnt Sienna. Walk out the brush well before applying paint. Cut out an egg template from a scrap of paper, using the egg pattern. Set over one egg. Using the toothbrush and Sable Brown, spatter over the egg shape. Remove the template and let dry. Flip the template, then repeat for other egg. Spatter the half-egg as well.

6 Create the Twigs

Using the no. 4 round stroke brush and Sable Brown, add the twigs. Use full pressure for the thick areas of the twigs and the point of the brush and light pressure for the finer twig ends. To shade, touch down in curved areas and in sections where the twigs split with Burnt Sienna. Add highlights on the opposite sides with a brush mix of Sable Brown plus a touch of Antique White. Remember to stop and start where twigs overlap to show depth.

7 Add the Little Leaves

Create little leaves with the no. 6 filbert and Light Avocado, pulling from the branch out. Group some in pairs, some in clusters of three, and leave some of the leaves single. The leaf sizes should vary. Paint smaller leaves toward the thinner end of the twig.

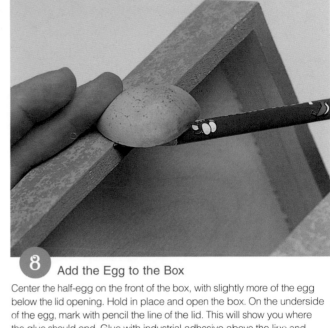

8 Add the Egg to the Box

Center the half-egg on the front of the box, with slightly more of the egg below the lid opening. Hold in place and open the box. On the underside of the egg, mark with pencil the line of the lid. This will show you where the glue should end. Glue with industrial adhesive above the line and attach to the box lid. A piece of scrap paper can be placed below the egg on the box bottom to prevent it from gluing the box shut. Lay the box on the hinged side and allow the glue to set. Sign your name, and apply sealant to finish (see tips on finishing, page 15).

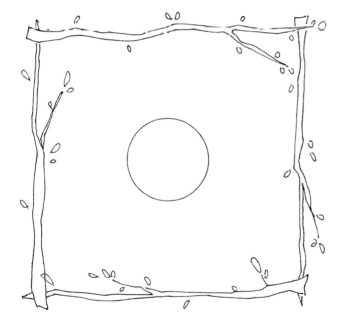

Egg and Twigs Enlarge at 140%

ENJOYING *the* HARVEST

At last, all of your hard work has paid off and it's time to reap the rewards! There are just a few more techniques left to learn. You'll then be able to combine your new knowledge of painting nature's treasures and beautifully textured backgrounds in combinations you never knew had been germinating inside of you all along.

This section is full of faux finishes to try your hand at. Wet-on-wet techniques, such as slip-slap and faux marble, gently blend one or more colors together to create true perfection. We'll even explore the use of plastic wrap to produce a wrinkled look that can be done with the plastic laid out flat or scrunched into a ball.

Mother Nature has supplied the inspiration; now it's up to you to bring her jewels to life indoors and to share your devotion to earthly treasures with those you love.

Aged to Perfection

Leaves have such an amazing texture of their own. I wanted to explore the possibility

of a painted texture becoming the leaf itself, rather than the background.

Isn't it amazing how a palette of just three colors combines to create such stunning results?

Materials

- rectangular plaque
- Faux Glazing Medium
- wood sealer
- no. 1 script liner
- ¾-inch (19mm) wash brush
- 1-inch (25mm) basecoater
- plastic wrap
- stylus
- white transfer paper
- leaf pattern (page 71)

DecoArt Americana Acrylic Paints

- Burnt Sienna
- Raw Umber
- Sable Brown

1 Prepare and Add Glaze Mixture

Prepare the plaque with sealer and Burnt Sienna (see Preparing a Wood Surface, page 10). Mix Faux Glazing Medium and Sable Brown in equal parts (a dime size of each) on the palette paper. The medium will give a transparency to the Sable Brown and will add depth. Use the 1-inch (25mm) basecoater brush and with a little more water than usual left on the brush, cover the entire surface with the mixture. While the paint is wet, take the plastic wrap and lay it over the painted surface, working it down well into the paint. See the sidebar on page 71 for more information.

2 Press and Adjust Plastic Wrap

With your fingers, smoosh the wrap around, and pat until you get a texture you like. There should be no long bubbles, but a variety of small and medium-sized ones.

3 Lift and Remove Plastic Wrap

Lift and remove the plastic wrap and set the plaque aside to dry. For demonstration purposes, a lighter color is used here to allow you to easily see the resulting texture. The use of Sable Brown will be slightly more subtle.

69

4 Basecoat Around the Transferred Leaf

Looking at the pattern left from the plastic wrap, decide the best placement of the leaf pattern. For example, there could be a major line that looks like the main vein of the leaf. Using white transfer paper and a stylus, transfer the leaf pattern to the plaque. Using the ¾-inch (19mm) wash brush and Raw Umber, paint in the background around the leaf. This may take a couple of coats. Leave the sides of the plaque Burnt Sienna. Let dry.

5 Slip-Slap the Background

Load the ¾-inch (19mm) wash brush with Burnt Sienna, and blot on a paper towel. Loosely slip-slap in a bit of this color to the background. The surface of the plaque is barely skimmed with the brush. Continue in a criss-cross fashion over the entire background to add color variations. Repeat in some areas for a brighter color.

6 Add the Leaf's Stem

Using the script liner, create a stem using Burnt Sienna. Add a Sable Brown highlight, using the same brush.

7 Pull the Leaf's Veins

Add a little water to some Raw Umber, then, using the script liner, add the leaf veins. Begin with the center vein. Pull secondary veins from the center vein and lastly, pull the most finely painted veins from the secondary veins.

8 Shade the Leaf

With the ¾-inch (19mm) wash brush, float Burnt Sienna on both sides of the center and secondary veins, but do not cross over any of these veins. Sign your name, and apply sealant to finish (see tips on finishing, page 15).

Leaf Enlarge at 145%

Plastic Wrap and Texture

When using the plastic wrap on a wet surface, I like to lay it flat and let the moisture pull at it. I then will move it around with my fingers to avoid getting a pattern with either a vertical or horizontal feel. By moving it, you will create more lines and bubbles, making the end result very interesting.

When balling up the plastic wrap, as in other projects, remember to pounce off excess paint first, then apply to your surface. Vary your hand movements so that you don't create an identifiable pattern.

71

"Hi" Stool

This little stool can be used in the house, in a garden room or even outdoors.

The design is delicate and charming and helps to make the stool a welcome addition for any room.

Materials

- wooden rectangular stepping stool
- Faux Glazing Medium
- wood sealer
- no. 4 round stroke brush
- no. 8 shader brush
- ¾-inch (19mm) wash brush
- 1-inch (25mm) basecoater
- old toothbrush
- plastic wrap
- wood glue
- hammer
- finishing nails
- stylus
- white transfer paper
- twig pattern (page 75)

DecoArt Americana Acrylic Paints

■	Antique Gold	■	Mississippi Mud
■	Celery Green	■	Mistletoe
■	Driftwood	■	Raw Umber
■	Forest Green	□	Titanium White
■	Midnite Green		

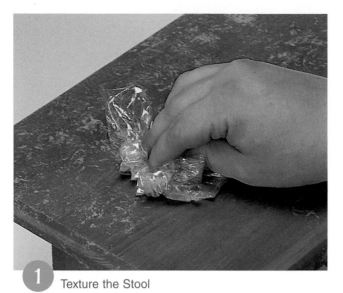

1 Texture the Stool

Sand all wood pieces and wipe with a damp paper towel. Assemble the stool following the manufacturer's directions with wood glue and finishing nails. Prepare the stool with sealer and Forest Green (see Preparing a Wood Surface, page 10). Mix three parts Mistletoe with one part Celery Green. Mix that with an equal amount of Faux Glazing Medium. Wad up a ball of plastic wrap, creating a lot of crinkles. Pounce this ball into the glazing mixture, then onto your palette paper to remove excess paint. Pounce paint onto the stool. Cover the entire stool with this texture. Remember to pounce onto the edges as well.

2 Spatter With Antique Gold

Transfer the "Hi" twig pattern image to the slight-left center of the top of the stool, using the stylus and the white transfer paper. Spatter the entire stool using the toothbrush and Antique Gold. It will appear bright when wet but will lighten as it dries. Cover the stool randomly, to suit your taste.

3 Basecoat the Twigs

Using the no. 4 round stroke brush and Mississippi Mud, basecoat the twigs. Use the point of the brush for the finer areas and press down on the brush for the wider areas. If the stool you are using is very grainy, more water may be necessary.

4 Shade the Twigs

Shade with Raw Umber to create depth and show that some twigs overlap other twigs. This is done with the ¾-inch (19mm) wash brush. Floats should be choppy, rather than smooth, to resemble bark texture.

Tip

When texturing with glazing medium, if you get too much paint in one area, take a second piece of plastic wrap and pounce over it lightly with the original basecoat color.

5 Add the Daisy Petals

On the opposite side of where the twigs were shaded, highlight them with Driftwood and the ¾-inch (19mm) wash brush. Remember to stop and start where the twigs overlap. To create the daisies, load the no. 8 shader fully with Titanium White, then stand it straight up on the chisel edge and tap down. Create petals by repeating in a circular motion. The more pressure that is applied, the fluffier the petals will be. Randomly place five daisies on the stool top and one on each side.

6 Create the Dandelions

Add centers to the daisies with the no. 4 round stroke brush and Antique Gold. Create dandelions in the same way as the daisies, but leave little, if any, space in between the petals, and use slightly more pressure to flare the outside of the brush. First make each flower with the no. 8 shader brush and Antique Gold. Highlight them with a brush mix of Antique Gold plus a touch of Titanium White. Brighten each flower with the same brush and just Titanium White.

7 Shade Behind the Twigs

Using the ¾-inch (19mm) wash brush and Midnite Green, shade in areas around the twigs where there is a natural curve or split in the twigs. This gives the twigs further dimension. Sign your name, and apply sealant to finish (see tips on finishing, page 15).

"HI" twig Enlarge at 134%

Variation

Papier-mâché Ornament

1. Base entire ornament with two coats of Celery Green. Once dry, base again. While the paint is wet, with the ¾-inch wash brush, slip-slap Forest Green on both the top and bottom, blending as you go. Let your brush strokes show for added interest. Paint the edges Forest Green. Float Forest Green along the top and bottom edges, using the wash brush, to deepen.
2. Freehand the letters with a charcoal pencil, then follow steps 3, 4, 5 and 7 to create the twigs and the daisies.
3. The dot on the "i" is made to look like a leaf. Base in with Forest Green, and highlight with Celery Green.
4. Follow steps 5 and 6 for the daisies.

"Tag, You're It"

I was so thrilled to find these wooden tags, and I knew various bugs

would look great on them. Mix and match, but most of all enjoy!

Materials

- wooden art tags set
- Faux Glazing Medium
- wood sealer
- no. 1 liner brush
- no. 4 round stroke brush
- ⅜-inch (10mm) DM Stippler brush
- ¾-inch (19mm) wash brush

- 1-inch (25mm) basecoater
- plastic wrap
- pencil
- stylus
- super chacopaper
- bug patterns (page 79)

DecoArt Americana Acrylic Paints

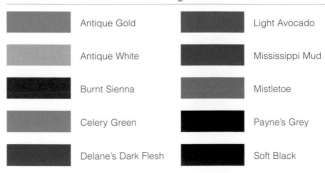

Antique Gold	Light Avocado
Antique White	Mississippi Mud
Burnt Sienna	Mistletoe
Celery Green	Payne's Grey
Delane's Dark Flesh	Soft Black

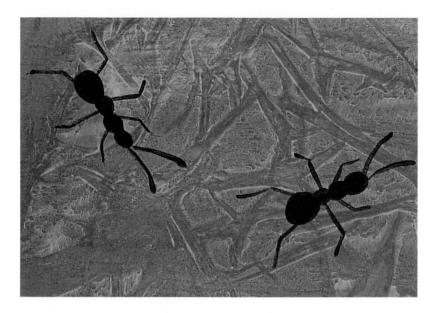

1. Basecoat the Ants

Gently punch out each tag, then sand lightly. Basecoat all of the tags with their own color, as follows, plus wood sealer. For the largest tag use Delane's Dark Flesh, for the medium tag use Mississippi Mud, for one small tag use Antique Gold and for the other use Celery Green. When dry, sand all the tags and apply a second basecoat of the appropriate color and dry again. Mix equal parts of Faux Glazing Medium and Antique White. Apply a coat to each with the 1-inch (25mm) basecoater. While wet, lay a piece of plastic wrap over each tag and smoosh it around with your fingers to create texture. Remove wrap and let dry. Begin with the large tag, and transfer the ant pattern to it using a stylus and the super chacopaper. Using the liner brush, basecoat the ants with Soft Black.

2. Shade the Ants

Using the ¾-inch (19mm) wash brush and Payne's Grey, shade the bottom of each ant. The bottom will be whichever side the ant is leaning towards. Highlight the ants with the ¾-inch (19mm) wash brush and Mississippi Mud on the opposite side of the shading.

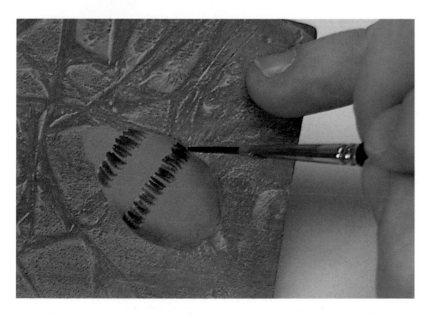

3. Add the Bee Stripes

Transfer the bees pattern to the medium tag with a stylus and the super chacopaper. Basecoat the bee bodies with Antique Gold and the ⅜-inch (10mm) DM Stippler. To shade the bodies, float Burnt Sienna down the sides of the bodies with the ¾-inch (19mm) wash brush. Using the liner and Soft Black, create stripes on the bodies with small, vertical lines. Thin the black with a little water if necessary to improve the flow of the paint.

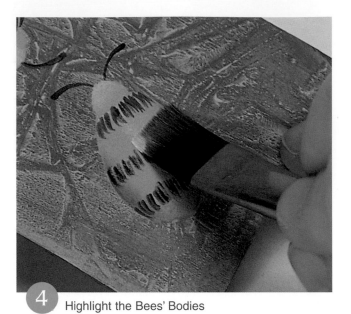

4 Highlight the Bees' Bodies

Add antenna with the liner and Soft Black. Pull from the outside in toward the head. Using the ¾-inch (19mm) wash brush, highlight the top of the head with Antique White. Create a shine spot highlight with Antique White down the center of the body by first dampening and then stroking on top.

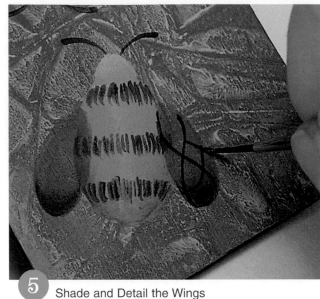

5 Shade and Detail the Wings

Using the no. 4 round stroke brush, basecoat the wings with Mississippi Mud. Shade the wing bottoms with Soft Black and the ¾-inch (19mm) wash brush. Using the liner, add veins of Soft Black.

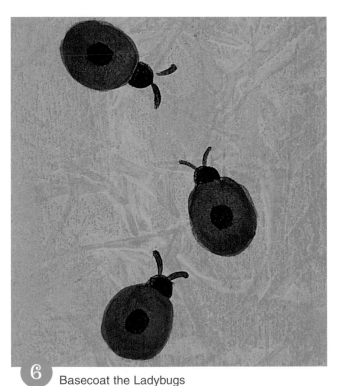

6 Basecoat the Ladybugs

Transfer the ladybug pattern to the Antique Gold small tag with super chacopaper and a stylus. Basecoat the wings with Burnt Sienna and the no. 4 round stroke brush. Make wing spots and the antennae with Soft Black and the liner.

7 Highlight the Wings and Heads

Highlight the wing and the head with Antique White using the ¾-inch (19mm) wash brush.

8 Create the Beetle

Transfer the beetle pattern to the Celery Green small tag with the super chacopaper and the stylus. Basecoat the beetle with the no. 4 round stroke brush and Payne's Grey. Pull the antennae with the liner. To highlight the body, float Light Avocado with the ¾-inch (19mm) wash brush. Highlight both eyes, the head, the top center of the back and the bottom of the wings as well as the tip of the tail with Light Avocado. Brighten the highlights with a thin float of Mistletoe and the ¾-inch (19mm) wash brush.

9 Add Highlights to Beetle's Back

Pull lines of Payne's Grey down the back using the liner. Wider lines are best. Add a brush mix of Payne's Grey and Antique White to highlight these same lines. Dot eyes with Antique White and the liner. Sign your name, and apply sealant to finish (see tips on finishing, page 15).

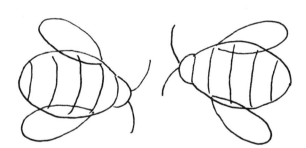

Bees *Reproduce at 100%*

Beetle *Reproduce at 100%*

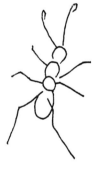

Ladybugs *Reproduce at 100%*

Ants *Reproduce at 100%*

Fall-Framed

When choosing a subject matter for this frame, I literally walked outside and grabbed two oak leaves. You could use your own leaves instead of the pattern, if you so desire.

Materials

- arch-top frame
- 2 wooden acorns
- Faux Glazing Medium
- wood sealer
- no. 1 script liner
- ¾-inch (19mm) wash brush
- 1-inch (25mm) basecoater
- stylus
- white transfer paper
- leaves pattern (page 81)
- industrial adhesive

DecoArt Americana Acrylic Paints

- Antique Gold
- Burnt Sienna
- Mississippi Mud
- Sable Brown
- Soft Black

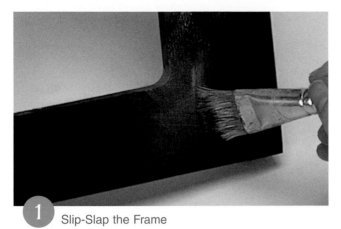

1 Slip-Slap the Frame

Prepare the frame with sealer and Soft Black (see Preparing a Wood Surface, page 10). While wet, slip-slap Burnt Sienna in three places and then Antique Gold in two places. Carry over to the frame edges. Let dry.

2 Basecoat the Leaves

Transfer the leaf patterns to the frame with white transfer paper and a stylus. Position each leaf as you see fit. Wrap a leaf that goes to the edge of the frame around the side. Using the ¾-inch (19mm) wash brush, basecoat the leaves and acorns with two coats of Mississippi Mud.

3 Pull the Leaves' Stems

Pull the stems with a script liner and Mississippi Mud. Create a palette of three dime-sized puddles of Faux Glazing Medium to: Sable Brown, Burnt Sienna, and a mixture of Mississippi Mud plus Soft Black. The ratio should be slightly more glazing medium than paint. Mix each well.

4 Create Crinkled Texture

Using the ¾-inch (19mm) wash brush and a little more water in the brush than normal, dab these colors randomly onto the leaves in short, quick strokes, one color at a time. Make three to five spots of each color. The goal is to create a crinkled, colorful tint to the leaves.

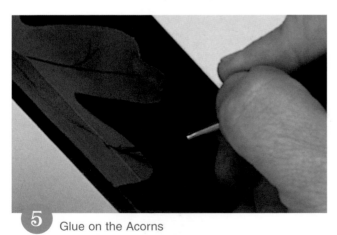

5 Glue on the Acorns

Give several spots of these mixes to the acorns, and set them aside. Mix equal parts of Soft Black and Faux Glazing Medium. Using the script liner, create the veins of the leaves, beginning with the center vein, then secondary veins, and finally the finer veins. Don't forget to carry veins over to the edges of the frame, where necessary. When dry, use industrial adhesive to glue on the acorns. Sign your name, and apply sealant to finish (see tips on finishing, page 15).

Leaves *Enlarge at 155%*

Feather Elegance

I wanted this piece to be upscale, elegant and stylized. By making it look marbleized,

the softness of the feather is a nice contradiction to the texture.

Materials

- wooden oval-opening frame
- Faux Glazing Medium
- wood sealer
- no. 1 script liner brush
- ⅜-inch (10mm) DM Stippler brush
- ¾-inch (19mm) wash brush
- 1-inch (25mm) basecoater
- sea sponge
- transparent tape
- T-square
- ruler
- pencil
- stylus
- super chacopaper
- white charcoal pencil
- feather pattern (page 85)

DecoArt Americana Acrylic Paints

- Antique White
- French Mocha
- Light Buttermilk
- Mocha
- Sable Brown

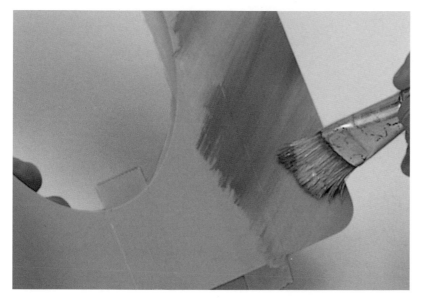

① Blend Mocha With French Mocha

Prepare the frame with sealer and Mocha (see Preparing a Wood Surface, page 10). Measure 3¼" (8cm) from the left and mark with the white charcoal pencil. Using a T-square, draw a vertical line at this mark. Make a second mark 2½" (6cm) from the first mark and draw a parallel line here. Tape both lines inward (the inner line of tape will go into the opening of the frame). Burnish down the tape well with your fingers. On the left side of the tape (toward the outside of the frame) basecoat Mocha over the entire section, using the 1-inch (25mm) basecoater. While wet, side load the brush with French Mocha and, keeping your strokes in a diagonal direction, blend the two colors together on your frame. Work quickly with a wetter-than-normal brush. Carry the color over to the sides.

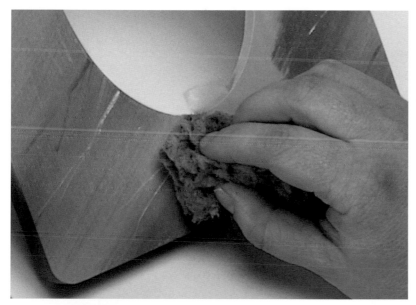

② Repeat Strokes on the Left Side

Repeat these two coats on the other side. Include the inner edge of the opening. Carry over the flow of the darker stripes from the first section to this section. Dry these sections well. Working on one side at a time, dampen the area with Faux Glazing Medium and the 1-inch (25mm) basecoater. Using the script liner, add a few diagonal marble lines with Light Buttermilk and a few lines of French Mocha. Pounce over the lines with a dampened sea sponge to soften.

③ Remove the Tape

Carefully remove the tape. If any paint seeped under the tape, clean it up with Mocha.

Tip

Nervous about trying a new technique? Try a "practice run" on the back or the bottom of the surface.

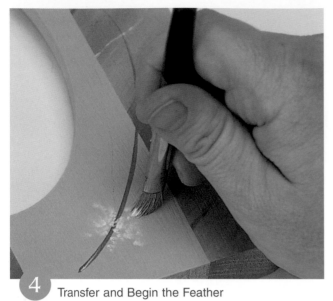

4 **Transfer and Begin the Feather**

Using the super chacopaper and the feather pattern, transfer the image with a stylus to the bottom right corner of the frame. Using the script liner, create the center vein of the feather with Sable Brown. Add a highlight to the bottom of the vein by loading the same brush with a touch of Antique White. For the downy area of the feather, use the DM Stippler brush and pounce Antique White from the center vein out.

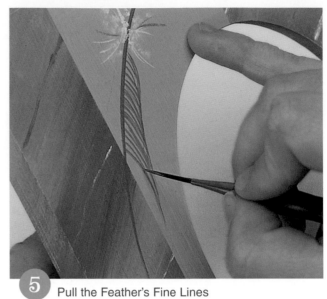

5 **Pull the Feather's Fine Lines**

With the script liner and Light Buttermilk, pull five or six fine strands from the center vein out in the downy section. Brush mix in Sable Brown and pull about three strokes in the same downy area. Using Sable Brown, thinned a bit with water, and the script liner, begin pulling the lines of the feather in a curved, graceful manner. You don't want them straight, or they will resemble an arrow.

6 **Curve the Top Lines**

As the lines get closer to the top of the feather, they are shorter, but still curved. Pull all lines from the center out.

7 **Shade the Feather**

Float Sable Brown lightly with the ¾-inch (19mm) wash brush in areas along the left outside of the feather and along the right side of the center vein.

8 Add the Highlight Lines

To highlight the feather, pull lines of Light Buttermilk with the script liner from the outside of the feather in.

9 Create a Shadow

Float Light Buttermilk in the highlighted area with the ¾-inch (19mm) wash brush. Float French Mocha with the same brush at the base of the feather to make a shadow. Remove any super chacopaper lines with a damp brush or cloth. Sign your name, and apply sealant to finish (see tips on finishing, page 15).

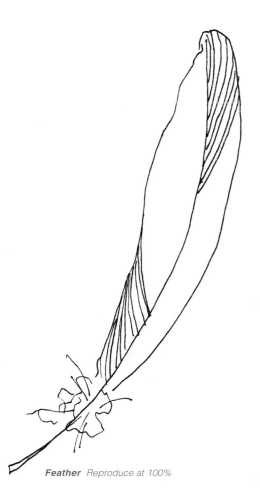

Feather *Reproduce at 100%*

Caught in Flight

This is my favorite piece in the book. The dragonfly is a much-loved subject of mine
and the texture on the frame only adds interest—it's a great combination.

Materials

- shadow box frame
- wooden plugs
- wooden dragonfly cutout
- Faux Glazing Medium
- wood sealer
- no. 1 script liner
- no. 10 shader brush
- ¾-inch (19mm) wash brush
- 1-inch (25mm) basecoater
- plastic wrap
- pencil
- stylus
- white transfer paper
- wood glue
- dragonfly pattern (page 89)

DecoArt Americana Acrylic Paints

- Celery Green
- French Mocha
- Light Avocado
- Light Buttermilk
- Soft Black

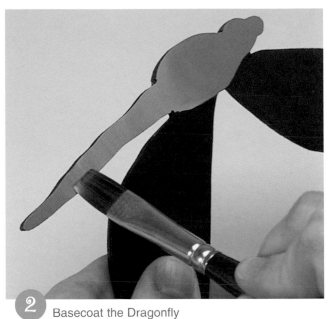

1 Add Basecoat and Texture to the Frame

Prepare the frame and dragonfly with sealer and Soft Black (see Preparing a Wood Surface, page 10). Mix Faux Glazing Medium and Light Avocado in equal parts. Apply this mixture generously to the top edges of the frame. While wet, lay a piece of plastic wrap over and press around with your fingers to form a pleasing pattern. Remove plastic wrap. Take another piece of wrap, wad into a ball, and dip into the mixture. Pounce off excess, and then pounce onto the thin side edges of the frame.

2 Basecoat the Dragonfly

Basecoat the dragonfly body, tail, legs and eyes with Light Avocado using the no. 10 shader brush. Basecoat the top surface only, not the edges. Apply a second coat of Light Avocado. When you begin to reach the tail section, pick up a bit of Celery Green and begin working in the color, in short strokes, then pick up French Mocha for the tip of the tail. Repeat to make both of the colors more opaque. It should be gradual with no stop and start lines, just a smooth transition from one color to the next.

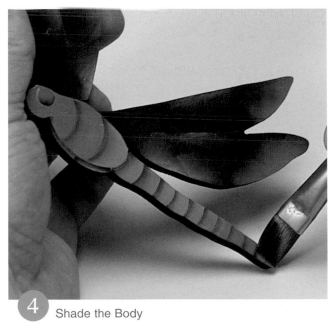

3 Float Color Onto the Wings

Using the ¾-inch (19mm) wash brush, loosely float Celery Green, Light Avocado and French Mocha onto the wings. The Light Avocado is closer to the tail and the Celery Green and the French Mocha are used more on the outer tips.

4 Shade the Body

Trace the eye and body detail from the pattern onto the dragonfly with the white transfer paper and a stylus. Shade the body and the tail segments with Soft Black, using the no. 10 shader brush.

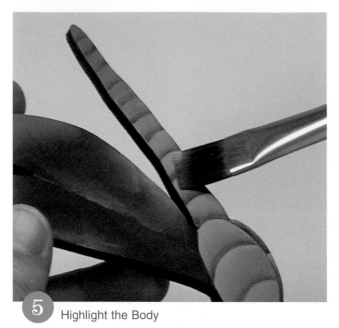

5 Highlight the Body

Highlight the body and the first few tail segments with the no. 10 shader brush and Celery Green.

6 Pull the Wing Details

Using the script liner and Light Buttermilk, pull the long detail veins in the wings. Also add highlights to the tops of the eyes.

7 Add Secondary Veins

In between each of the main wing veins, create many smaller veins. Begin with irregular "X" shapes between two lines using a script liner and Light Buttermilk.

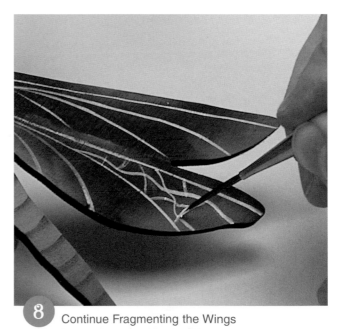

8 Continue Fragmenting the Wings

Break up these sections into smaller segments. Continue fragmenting throughout all of the wing area.

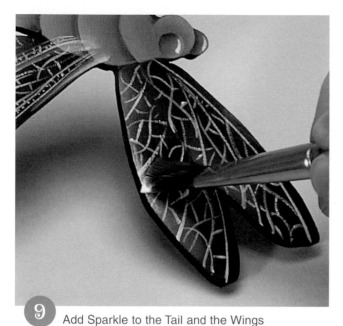

9 Add Sparkle to the Tail and the Wings

Float Light Buttermilk for sparkle to the base of the tail and on the centers of the inner edges of the wings, using the no. 10 shader brush.

10 Add the Dragonfly to the Frame

Base the wooden plugs with Soft Black and glue them to the back of the dragonfly with wood glue. Then glue the dragonfly into the frame. Sign your name, and apply sealant to finish (see tips on finishing, page 15).

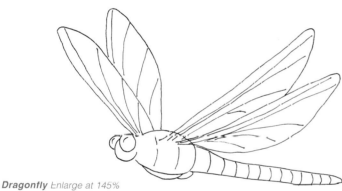

***Dragonfly** Enlarge at 145%*

Variation

Trinket Basket

1. Cut a lid out of 1/2" (13mm) wood to fit a dollar store wire basket. Make sure to instep the bottom 1/4" (6mm) so it will stay on the basket top.
2. Basecoat the lid with Soft Black.
3. Follow step 1 to add texture, except mix French Mocha with the Faux Glazing Medium, instead of Light Avocado.
4. Basecoat the dragonfly body with Celery Green. Shade to the right of all body segments and bottom with Light Avocado. Brush mix Celery Green plus Light Buttermilk for highlights.
5. Paint eyes with Light Avocado, and highlight with Celery Green. Put a comma stroke in with Light Buttermilk for sparkle.
6. Deepen eyes, body segments (not tail) and bottom of body and tail with a brush mix of Light Avocado plus Soft Black.
7. Wash over the wings with Light Buttermilk. Separate with a float of Soft Black. Create veins with watery Soft Black. Shade here and there with soft floats of Soft Black. Outline the wings with Light Buttermilk, using a wavy hand.

Every-Birdy's Welcome

This charming piece would look great by a door, hanging on a wall or given as a gift. As you can see, the possibilities are endless.

Materials

- wooden oval sign plaque
- Faux Glazing Medium
- wood sealer
- no. 1 liner brush
- no. 2 flat brush
- no. 6 filbert brush
- ¾-inch (19mm) wash brush
- 1-inch (25mm) basecoater
- plastic wrap
- stylus
- graphite paper
- letters, twig and feather pattern (page 93)

DecoArt Americana Acrylic Paints

Antique White	Light Avocado
Burnt Sienna	Light Buttermilk
Celery Green	Midnite Green
French Mocha	Mississippi Mud

1 Add Texture and Letters to Oval

Prepare oval with sealer and Celery Green (see Preparing a Wood Surface, page 10). Sand lightly, then mix equal parts of Faux Glazing Medium and Antique White. Using the 1-inch (25mm) basecoater brush, apply this mixture to the front of the sign. Lay a piece of plastic wrap over the wet paint mixture. Move the wrap around and press it down in places with your fingers. Gently remove the wrap to reveal the texture. Let dry. Transfer the pattern to the front of the sign with graphite paper and a stylus, centering as you wish. Mix equal parts of Light Avocado and Midnite Green. Outline the letters with the liner brush, then fill the letters in.

2 Add the Branches Box

Form the branches of the box shape with the liner and Mississippi Mud. Pull out additional freehand branches from the box shape according to the shape of your sign. Add a few or several branches depending on how full you like it. Pull lines of Burnt Sienna in a few areas to shade with the liner. Use Antique White in a few areas to highlight.

3 Add the Leaves and Basecoat the Bird

Add Light Avocado leaves with the no. 6 filbert, pulling from the branch out. Make additional leaves with Midnite Green. Basecoat the bird body with French Mocha and the no. 2 flat brush. Basecoat the wing with a brush mix of French Mocha plus a touch of Light Buttermilk. Using the liner and Burnt Sienna, add the feet and the beak.

4 Shade and Highlight the Bird

Shade the base of the body with Burnt Sienna and the ¾-inch (19mm) wash brush. Highlight the wing with a brush mix of French Mocha and a bit more Light Buttermilk than was used on the basecoat, using the ¾-inch (19mm) wash brush. Add three comma strokes of French Mocha to make the tail of the bird. Make an eye for the bird with the liner brush and the mixture used for the lettering. Add a highlight dot of Light Buttermilk.

5 Create the Feather's Vein and Down

Use the liner and Mississippi Mud to form the center vein of the feather. Add a highlight at the base of the vein with Light Buttermilk. Pull about a 1" (3cm) line of the lettering mix ¼" (6mm) up from the base of the vein to create a shadow. Create the downy section of the feather by tapping the liner up and down, using a brush mix of Mississippi Mud and Light Buttermilk. With Light Buttermilk, stipple in a few highlights on the top of the downy section.

6 Pull Feather Hairs and Highlights

Pull a few stray hairs from each color in the downy area with the liner. Stroke the feather on using Mississippi Mud. Keep the strokes curved, rather than straight, or you will end up with an arrow. Pull highlights with Light Buttermilk from the outside of the feather in toward the center vein. Create a concentrated area of Light Buttermilk in the top left section.

7 Add the Feather's Spot

Using the lettering mix and the liner, create a spot over the concentrated Light Buttermilk area by pulling strokes that follow the highlight lines, but still creating a round shape for a spot on the feather.

8 Shade the Feather

Float Mississippi Mud with the ¾-inch (19mm) wash brush to shade on the outer left of the feather and the right of the center vein. Add a float of Burnt Sienna in a few places for depth. Using the ¾-inch (19mm) wash brush, add Midnite Green to the outside edge of the sign. Sign your name, and apply sealant to finish (see tips on finishing, page 15).

Letters, twig and feather Enlarge at 110%

Resources

Paints & Mediums

DecoArt
PO Box 386
Stanford, KY 40484
www.decoart.com
(800) 367-3047

Surfaces

Walnut Hollow
1409 State Road 23
Dodgeville, WI 53533
www.walnuthollow.com
(800) 950-5101
Scallop Frame (23420)
Heart Plaque (24086)
9.5" Plate (3523)
Arch Frame (23421)
Frame with Oval Opening (23414)
Small Arch Clock (53201)
Clock Movement (TQ701B)
Rectangle Stool (9749)
Memory Frame (23877)
Oval Signboard (23870)
Personal Box (3209)

Painter's Paradise
Jo C. & Co.
C-10, 950 Ridge Road
Claymont, DE 19703
www.paintersparadise.com
(302) 798-3897
Tin Cup (810005)
13" Hobnail Plate (892466)

Cabin Crafters
1225 W. First Street
Nevada, IA 50201
www.cabincrafters.com
(800) 669-3920
Round Coaster Set (38-605)

Kelly Hoernig's Painted Stuff
15927 South Grove Road
Hebron, IN 46341
(219) 996-7714
Bee Cutout
Dragonfly Cutout

Lara's Crafts
www.larascrafts.com
Acorns (10643)
Let's Play Tag! Tag Set (PT1001)
Pigeon Egg Halves (10120)

Brushes & General Supplies

Loew-Cornell
563 Chestnut Avenue
Teaneck, NJ 07666
www.loewcornell.com
(800) 922-0186
All brushes
Brush Tub II (386)
Double-Ended Stylus (DES)
Palette Paper (398)
Fine Sanding Sponge (12338)
Fine/Medium Sanding Block (12336)
Fine Angled Sanding Block (12351)
Graphite Transfer Paper (392)
White Transfer Paper (394)
Super Chacopaper (738)
Sea Wool Sponge (497)
Compressed Sponges (39)

Delta Technical Coatings, Inc.
2550 Pellissier Place
Whittier, CA 90601
www.deltacrafts.com
(800) 423-4135
www.cthruruler.com
One-Step Background Stencils.
   Chintz (95 861 1013)
   Polka Dot (95 851 1013)
Stencil Sponges (60 510 0008)

The C-Thru Ruler Company
6 Britton Drive
Bloomfield, CT 06002
(800) 243-8419
18" Grid Ruler (B-85)
Jr. T-Square (JR-12)

Index

The best in creative crafting and decorative painting is from North Light Books!

Inspired by the Garden

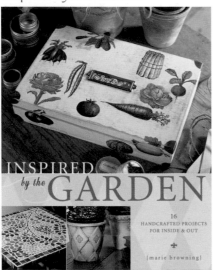

Inspired by the Garden presents 12 garden-inspired projects for inside and out. Using a range of crafting techniques and materials, this book showcases fun yet sophisticated garden décor projects perfect for crafters of all skill levels. Featuring popular garden motifs, projects include mosaic garden tables, matching pots and watering can, cards made with pressed flowers, a garden apron and more! ISBN 1-58180-434-2, paperback, 128 pages, #32630-K

Painting Garden Décor With Donna Dewberry

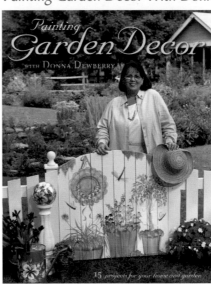

Transform your everyday outdoor furnishings into stunning, hand-painted garden accents. Acclaimed decorative painter Donna Dewberry shows you how to transform 15 deck, porch and patio pieces into truly lovely garden décor. Donna's easy-to-master brushwork techniques make each one fun and rewarding. No green thumb required! ISBN 1-58180-144-0, paperback, 144 pages, #31889-K

Handpainted Gifts for All Occasions

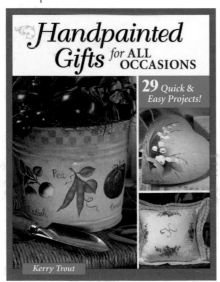

Celebrate the seasons, holidays and family events with 25 quick and easy painting projects. You'll find gifts for all of your family and friends, most of which can be made in an afternoon or less. Easy-to-follow instructions and step-by-step photos make it easy for you to create delightful projects for Mother's Day, Christmas, a new baby and more! ISBN 1-58180-426-1, paperback, 144 pages, #32590-K

Painting Garden Animals with Sherry C. Nelson

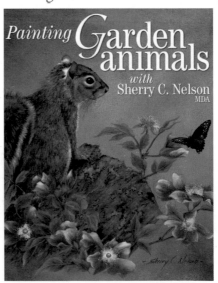

Learn Sherry C. Nelson's innovative and creative techniques for painting all of your favorite garden animals! Through 10 step-by-step exercises, Nelson will guide you to master each part of the animal including its eyes, nose, ears and paws, as well as painting realistic fur with distinctive color, markings and length. ISBN 1-58180-427-X, paperback, 144 pages, #32591-K

These and other fine North Light titles are available from your local arts and crafts retailer, bookstore, online supplier or by calling 1-800-448-0915.